KU-279-002

COACHING THE YOUNG DEVELOPING PERFORMER

Tracking Physical Growth and Development to Inform Coaching Programmes

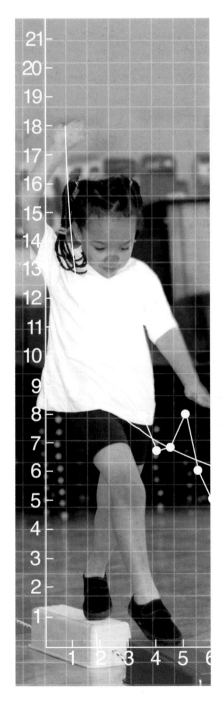

WITHDRAWN

LIVERPOOL JMU LIBRARY

3 1111 01327 4731

© The National Coaching Foundation, 2009

This resource is copyright under the Berne Convention. All rights are reserved. Apart from any fair dealing for the purposes of private study, research, criticism or review, as permitted under the Copyright, Designs and Patents Act 1988, no part of this publication may be reproduced, stored in a retrieval system, or transmitted in any form or by any means, electronic, electrical, chemical, mechanical, optical, photocopying, recording or otherwise, without the prior written permission of the copyright owner. Enquiries should be addressed to **Coachwise Business Solutions.**

sports coach UK is the brand name of The National Coaching Foundation
and has been such since April 2001.

ISBN: 978-1-905540-37-2

Authors
Istvan Balyi and Craig Williams

Contributors
Graham Ross (Chapters 3 and 4), Ian Stafford (Chapters 1 and 7),
Craig Williams (Chapter 2), Anne Pankhurst (Chapter 5), Brent Hills (Chapter 5),
Dawn Scott (Chapter 5) and Misia Gervis (Chapter 5)

Technical Editor
Anne Pankhurst

sports coach UK Support Team
Graham Ross, Heather Moir and Mark Drummond

Coachwise editorial and design team
Craig Smith and Ian Bolton

The authors and publishers would like to thank the following for their technical expertise in the review of this book: Ian Freeman (British Swimming), Martin Redden (British Gymnastics) and Steve Boocock (NSPCC Child Protection in Sport Unit).

While every effort has been made to trace and seek permission from copyright holders, the publishers, Coachwise Business Solutions, invite any unacknowledged copyright holders to email enquiries@coachwisesolutions.co.uk
It is the publisher's intent to fully credit any unacknowledged copyright holders at the earliest opportunity.

Front cover photographs © Alan Edwards and Andrew Couldridge/Action Images Limited

All other photographs © The National Coaching Foundation

Coachwise Business Solutions

sports coach UK
114 Cardigan Road
Headingley
Leeds LS6 3BJ
Tel: 0113-274 4802 Fax: 0113-275 5019
Email: coaching@sportscoachuk.org
Website: www.sportscoachuk.org

Patron: HRH The Princess Royal

Produced on behalf of sports coach UK by

Coachwise Business Solutions
Chelsea Close
Off Amberley Road
Armley
Leeds LS12 4HP
Tel: 0113-231 1310 Fax: 0113-231 9606

Email: enquiries@coachwisesolutions.co.uk
Website: www.coachwisesolutions.co.uk

Throughout this resource the terms *performer*, *player* and *athlete* are interchangeable and are intended to be inclusive of all sports.

The term *parent* includes carers, guardians and the other next of kin categories.

The term *Long-term Athlete Development (LTAD)* is intended to include players or any other sport-specific version of what a participant is in terms of paddler, fighter etc.

sports coach UK will ensure it has professional and ethical values and that all its practices are inclusive and equitable.

081033

Author Biographies

Istvan Balyi

Istvan Balyi is one of the world's leading experts on planning and periodisation, and on short- and long-term training, competition and recovery programming. Istvan has a depth of knowledge relating to the key factors involved in developing sporting potential and performance, together with practical experience, across a wide range of countries and sports. He has designed, implemented and monitored high-performance training, competition and recovery programmes for gold, silver, and bronze medallists at several Olympic Games and World Championships, in both winter and summer sports.

Assoc. Prof. Craig Williams

Craig Williams is an Associate Professor at the University of Exeter and is co-director of the Children's Health and Exercise Research Centre (CHERC). He has been involved in the teaching, coaching and research of children's health, physical activity and sport for over 20 years. Craig publishes regularly in a variety of peer-reviewed scientific journals, magazines and newspapers. He established and was the first convenor of the special interest group Paediatric Exercise Science for the British Association of Sport and Exercise Sciences (BASES). Research study outcomes have been disseminated to such organisations as the British Cycling Federation (BCF), British Gymnastics Association (BGA), the England and Wales Cricket Board (ECB) and several Premier League football clubs.

Graham Ross

Graham is a Senior Coaching Consultant with sports coach UK, responsible for leading the participant development work area. He has previously been Sports Development Manager at Sport England (1996–2005), where he lead the Long-term Athlete Development (LTAD) and Sports System Building project that was piloted with many leading governing bodies of sport. Prior to this, he was National Development Officer for Scottish Athletics (1992–1996).

Graham initially trained and worked as a physical education teacher, before moving into local authority sports development and facility management with Staffordshire County Council and Cardiff City Council. He holds a BA Honours in Geography from Birmingham University and a Certificate in Education (Physical Education and Geography) from Loughborough University. He also has a Diploma in Management Studies from Staffordshire University.

In addition, Graham has experience of teaching and coaching a wide variety of sports, but his main interest and focus as a coach, coach educator and coach manager has been in athletics. His athletics coaching experience covers a wide range of events from beginner to representative standard and he has coached athletes of international standard in various endurance events. Graham has been invited to speak at several national and international conferences on his experiences in setting up and implementing various athlete/player development programmes under the banner of the LTAD and Sports System Building project.

Ian Stafford

Ian is the Director of Coaching System Development at sports coach UK. He has previously been Head of Coach Education and served as a national trainer and senior tutor for sports coach UK for many years.

Ian initially trained and worked as a secondary school physical education teacher before moving into further education/higher education. He lectured at three different universities (approximately 25 years in total of HE), working on initial teacher education programmes and sport degrees.

He holds a Masters in Education from the University of Bristol and, prior to the UK Coaching Certificate, was an RFU senior coach and an English Volleyball Association club coach. Ian's coaching experience in both rugby union and volleyball covers a wide range at both club and representative levels with juniors and seniors, as well as HE students.

He has published articles in peer-reviewed journals and authored *Coaching for Long-term Athlete Development*. Most recently, he has been programme leader for a sports degree at Durham University, before moving to work full-time for sports coach UK.

Anne Pankhurst

Anne, until recently, worked as Manager of Coaching Education for the United States Tennis Association (USTA) with national and high-performance coaches and young talented players, providing them with information and resources to help develop future champions. Previously, she spent a year training coaches and developing programmes in a Texas tennis academy. For 10 years, prior to working in the US, Anne was the Coach Education Director for the Lawn Tennis Association. She was a member of the International Tennis Federation International Coaches Commission from 1997–2004 and has been a member of the United States Olympic Committee Coaching Education working party. Anne has been a presenter at numerous conventions and symposiums around the world.

A qualified physical education teacher and previously a full-time tennis coach, Anne studied part-time to gain a BA (Honours) in Developmental Geography. In addition, she has diplomas in advanced sports coaching, biomechanics and sports physiology. Anne is the author of three tennis coaching books and has written many articles on tennis coaching and the development of young athletes. In addition, she works as a technical editor for coach education resources, the two most recent being *Planning and Periodisation* and *An Introduction to the FUNdamentals of Movement*, for sports coach UK. She has also designed athlete development models for a number of different sports in the UK and the US, and is technical editor of *coaching edge*.

Contents

Preface

Ian Stafford

This book is aimed at practitioners, coaches and other support staff who work with, and develop training and competitive programmes for, young developing performers. It is written primarily for coaches of dedicated, competitive performers, although some concepts apply to a wider range of participants, such as recreational performers. Apart from practising coaches, interested readers could also include coach educators, managers, sports administrators and leaders. All these people, particularly coaches, will help ensure that taking part in sport really does provide the many physical, psychological and social benefits to young people we have all heard and talked about. With potential physical benefits of sport well-documented, the psychological and social benefits, although more difficult to estimate and substantiate, are at the heart of many sport-based programmes that target specific groups and different social issues.

One of the issues always raised when discussing the value of participation in sport is that for every benefit identified, an equal and opposite problem could arise. For example, the character-building nature of sport has long been seen as an important value. Conversely, research shows that, in certain circumstances, sport can encourage a win-at-all-costs attitude. Even in terms of the physical benefits of sport, there has been some debate. Participation in sport is generally considered a healthy pursuit, but many training and performance activities may actually lead to health problems, particularly in terms of overuse or misuse injuries. This seemingly negative statement about sport in a book about sports coaching may seem surprising, and readers may wonder why this issue has been highlighted from the outset. However, throughout this book, it will be clear this controversy actually serves to underline the importance of the long-term athlete/player development (LTAD) approach and reinforces the importance of logical, well-structured and progressive programmes that are built around the developmental stage of the young performer. LTAD is a structured and phased guide for the development of children, players and performers, both in participation and sports performance. It also provides a framework for the development of movement literacy among children, which underpins lifelong participation in sport and physical activity.

The principal intention of this book is to help coaches understand the developmental factors in young performers that can influence the planning and implementation of appropriate training and performance programmes. This understanding is fundamental if young performers are to be given the best opportunity to achieve their potential and personal excellence, with minimum opportunity for physical problems to be encountered along the way. Focus will be on how to establish relatively simple monitoring procedures that help coaches assess where their young performers are in terms of physical development. This allows for coaches to be better placed to plan and implement developmentally appropriate programmes. A fundamental intention of *Coaching the Young Developing Performer* is to examine the research and scientific data, combining it with evidence gained from practical experience of coaching young performers.

The term 'personal excellence' is used as a way of expanding on the concept of people achieving their potential in sport. If more people achieved their true potential, it seems logical to assume performance would improve at all levels. Nationally, it is important to produce successful performers at the highest level, but is it possible to produce performers who can achieve internationally, on a world stage, without effective training and competition programmes that support their development? In almost every sport, it is difficult to imagine a performer or team winning a medal at the Olympic Games, Paralympic Games or Commonwealth Games, without having undertaken a substantial and effective training, competition and recovery programme for a number of years. The planning and execution of appropriate training and competition goals and programmes is, therefore, essential to performers achieving personal excellence, and in keeping them motivated to continue striving for improvement.

With appropriate and quality programmes in place, the likelihood of young performers experiencing sport-related health problems should be minimised, and the chances of them achieving their goals increased. The aim of coaching for long-term athlete/player development is to improve both participation and performance in sport. If we accept lifelong participation can help develop a whole range of valuable skills and attributes, then an approach that helps keep young people involved in sport for longer and maximises their chances of achieving their true potential, including performing at the highest levels, must be encouraged.

Keeping more people active in sport for longer and the improvement of performance levels are naturally interlinked. A large dropout rate has been noted in many sports where young people have participated competitively as teenagers. Of course, many factors can have a bearing on this. The possibility cannot be ignored that some of this dropout may be related to the ineffective way young people have been developed and the inappropriate activities they may have experienced. An effective talent identification and development infrastructure will result in a larger base of participants from which to select. It will also have a consequent positive effect on overall performance. If performance levels are raised, more role models are produced, sports develop higher profiles, and more children and young people may be motivated to participate. So, the twin aspirations of increasing participation and improving performance should never be seen as an either/or situation. Rather, each should be seen as a fundamental ingredient of the other.

Readers of *Coaching the Young Developing Performer* will benefit from background knowledge, particularly in relation to LTAD and periodisation – the way in which a programme is divided into units, blocks or cycles, with appropriate periods of training, competition and recovery. A list of useful references will be found at the end of each chapter. In the sports coach UK LTAD series, a useful resource would be the *Preparing for a Life in Sport* leaflet (sports coach UK, 2004). The concept of peak height velocity (PHV) was raised in *Coaching for Long-term Athlete Development: to improve participation and performance in sport* (Stafford, 2005): this book serves as a useful introduction to this area. Additionally, it will offer information and advice for coaches to help them understand the key issues of training and the impact of the onset of PHV, and PHV itself, on young male and female performers in different age groups. Its intention is to extend the understanding of PHV and act as a bridge to *Planning and Periodisation* (Pankhurst, 2007). This process should help coaches and other support personnel use the information gained on tracking the physical development of their young athletes to plan an appropriately periodised programme. Throughout the book, there are many references to research and discussion papers, so coaches have the opportunity to study specific issues in more detail.

Coaching the Young Developing Performer has been produced with the aim of helping coaches further their understanding of coaching children and young performers through the growing, developing years. As outlined earlier, the focus is on the monitoring of young performers' growth and development in order to plan and implement appropriate training and competition programmes. This book will help coaches and other support staff recognise the opportunities this information gives them, both to develop the potential of more performers, and to give every performer the best deal. To make a real difference, coaches must not only further their knowledge and understanding in this area, but actually **apply** their learning in practice for the optimal benefit of their young performers.

Chapter 1: **Introduction**

Ian Stafford

As young people grow, develop and mature into adult performers, many important changes take place. Most obvious are the physical changes, but the psychological, social and emotional changes, while not so evident or directly observable, are equally important for coaches to understand and consider. What will be familiar to the coach are the changes in behaviour accompanying psychological, social and emotional development, particularly at key times, such as at puberty and during adolescence. These factors should also be given consideration. Supporting the long-term development of performers in an effective way is a particularly challenging part of a coach's role, and one which requires coaches and other support staff to have every tool at their disposal. The following information is essential to the process of supporting young, developing performers both within and through sport.

The development of young people, from birth to adulthood, follows a pattern that experienced coaches will have noted across a large number of performers. However, a specific and individual development pathway will be needed to maximise the quality of experience and ultimate performance level of every individual performer. Long-term athlete/player development (LTAD) addresses the issue of chronological age being a relatively poor indicator of the maturation process that takes place as an individual grows and develops. Every coach will be able to recite anecdotes of performers of the same chronological age who exhibit great differences in their levels of maturity, especially during puberty. At present, however, the physical development of children and young performers is

much easier to track and monitor than the other aspects of development identified above. In addition, the physical changes and other indicators of maturation do have major, direct implications for the training and competition loads, and programmes, that coaches set for their young performers. Having highlighted the importance of all aspects of individual development, it is acknowledged this resource does not adopt a holistic approach. Rather, it focuses on helping coaches use the more accessible methods of monitoring young people's individual physical growth to guide programme planning and implementation.

LTAD, much of which is based on the work of Istvan Balyi, aims to offer a long-term approach to maximising individual potential and involvement in sport. It is one of a number of models highlighting key, common principles of player/performer development. LTAD has been a key driver in challenging governing bodies of sport and related organisations to consider the meaning of good practice, in terms of the planning and coaching processes needed for young performers to flourish. It is intended to produce a long-term perspective to maximise individual potential and involvement in sport.

As with other resources in the LTAD suite, certain principles and messages will be highlighted throughout *Coaching the Young Developing Performer*. The key principles and core values that underpin the LTAD approach are set out below. Although some repetition and overlap will be noted, this only serves to reinforce the fundamental messages of the LTAD framework.

Core Values

1. LTAD acknowledges that each child, player and performer is different, with individual needs and rates of development.
Before applying LTAD to programme design and coaching, it is essential the principle of individual difference and progression is understood and accepted. Such understanding and acceptance will maximise the effective application of the model in line with the needs of the child, player and performer.

2. LTAD provides a framework for planning and decision making on performer development. This is not a rigid template.
Once the principles of individual differences and progression have been accepted, LTAD provides a clear framework for planning the development of performers and setting out of appropriate programmes. The framework provides the basis on which decisions concerning performer needs and state of readiness can be made.

3. LTAD is concerned with the holistic development of children, players and performers, including movement literacy, technical, tactical, physical, mental, personal and lifestyle capabilities.
Such development is part of a complex and interrelated process, whereby each capability develops at different rates within, and among, individuals.

4. LTAD stages overlap and are unique to each individual.
Progression through the stages of LTAD will be unique to each individual, with elements of one stage overlapping with the next. Diagnostic tools are needed to track the development of children, players and performers related to each capability at every stage. Compensatory activities may be needed to address deficits that have carried over from one stage to the next.

5. LTAD recognises the significance of transitions in the development of children, players and performers.
By highlighting clear stages, LTAD provides a basis for identifying and planning key transitions in the development of children, players and performers as they progress, at their own rate, from one stage to the next.

6. LTAD recognises the accumulation of deliberate practice and training age is linear and the development of key capabilities is non-linear and individualised.
LTAD is based on the assumption that the development of sport expertise requires the substantial accumulation of deliberate practice over time, which, in turn, forms the basis for training age (general and sport specific). While the accumulation of practice can be plotted in a linear way, the quality and effects of such practice are more complex, non-linear and different for each individual.

Key Principles

- The nature of the growing child in terms of the stage of development is a central consideration when planning and implementing coaching programmes.

- Different sports require the specialisation of young people at an early age or later. This is fundamental in determining training and competition programmes.

- FUNdamental skills and the movement literacy acquired during a child's early sport experiences are of vital importance for subsequent development.

- Training windows appear at different times during maturation. These are the sensitive times at which certain types of training can be particularly beneficial. Sensitive periods must be fully appreciated and exploited for optimal training effect, and to help young performers realise their true potential.

- As coaches, we need to review our competition and training programmes for young performers. More innovative and creative thinking is required, along with a revision of the competitive experiences we set for young performers.

- The wider role of the coach plays a significant part in terms of involving key people, such as parents, teachers, administrators, fixture secretaries and officials, to produce an integrated and progressive sports experience for young people.

- System integration is vital. There is a need to unify everything for young performers in terms of their sports experience in schools and clubs, coaching programmes, coach education, competitive structures and appropriate support systems.

- Approximately 10 years of intensive practice is required to excel in anything. If potential is to be realised, there are no shortcuts.

- There exists a commitment to continuous improvement. The LTAD model should reflect good coaching practice in terms of being constantly reviewed and improved in light of research evidence and changing environments.

The last bullet point above should be borne in mind when reading this resource. The principles, practices and key messages throughout are currently considered best practice. However, as continuous improvement is at the heart of LTAD, the present model is evolving and will be constantly reviewed and progressed in light of new research, changing sporting environments and the direct experiences of coaches.

In previous LTAD publications, the value of the approach to both improving participation – keeping more young people active for longer – and enhancing performance, at all levels, has been highlighted. *Coaching the Young Developing Performer* is aimed at coaches working within a more competitive environment. For example, on talent identification and development programmes in academies, centres of excellence or with representative squads. This is not to say coaches working at club or development level will not find the resource useful. However, it is acknowledged the time and resources needed to monitor physical development effectively are more likely to be available to coaches working within the performance arena.

With the 2012 Olympic Games and Paralympic Games being awarded to London, and the 2014 Commonwealth Games to be staged in Glasgow, much time and attention will be given to UK sport in the coming years to identify and develop young performers with the potential not only to be selected for these competitions, but to achieve medal-winning performances. Coaches currently working with talented young performers may well be coaching one or more individuals with such potential. Careful thought must be given to the way in which these performers are prepared in the years ahead, so they can achieve levels of personal excellence that ultimately allow for success at the highest level. The information in this resource expands on a number of key factors that contribute to the bigger picture of performer development. Each factor provides clear guidance to coaches working with young performers. However, the combination of these factors with a thorough understanding of their relationship to each other, gives coaches direction on how to develop individual programmes of training and competition for each young, developing performer.

The link between sport and health was identified in the preface, as was the issue of equal and opposites that may arise through taking part in sport: the problems of misuse and overuse injuries being given as examples. From the outset, coaches must have a sound philosophy on which to base their behaviour and practice. Tension exists between ensuring young sports performers develop as individuals in the most beneficial manner, while also guaranteeing they are given every opportunity to compete to their full potential and the highest possible level. Undoubtedly, some of the activities and practices currently engaged in to develop high-level performers are contentious in terms of their potential long-term effects on physical health. While outside the main focus of the resource, some may argue the amount of time aspiring high-level performers need to devote to their sport in developing years, may also have a detrimental effect on psychological and social development.

Coaches should be aware of this issue and ensure they fully understand the duty of care that exists in their working relationships with young performers. The fundamental principle of ethically sound coaching will be reinforced throughout and should be applied in all coaching plans and programmes. If such an approach to coaching is not demonstrated, parents will not entrust their children to coaches. Young performers will generally vote with their feet and move to a coach who has their interests at heart: as individuals and not just sports performers. The worst-case scenario is that talented young performers may have such a bad experience, under an unethical coaching regime, that they drop out of sport completely. Sport cannot afford to lose such gifted youngsters from its talent pool. So, while striving to produce the best from young performers, coaches must never lose sight of the fact they are working with young, growing and developing bodies – and impressionable young people. This privilege is a huge responsibility that should not be taken lightly.

The welfare of the young person must be at the heart of everything undertaken in coaching. Performer-centred coaching must be more than just an aspiration or a principle that resides in resources and coach education programmes. It must guide the planning of programmes and be reflected in all coaching behaviours and practices. Again, the aim of *Coaching the Young Developing Performer* is to help coaches gain knowledge and understanding to enable the planning of programmes developmentally appropriate in terms of training and competition loads their performers experience. In matching the activities and intensity of programmes to the performer's developmental stage, coaches are helping to ensure there is a greater chance of providing optimum benefit, and less chance of young performers incurring either physical or psychological health problems. To plan developmentally appropriate programmes, coaches require good background knowledge and experience of child growth and development. Much of this information is set out in other resources, such as *Coaching for Long-term Athlete Development: to improve participation and performance in sport* (Stafford, 2005) and *Coaching Young Performers* (Hagger, 2005). A major issue for coaches is chronological age being the main determinant of competition systems for young people in sport, while biological development may

vary considerably within any one age group. Related to this, the discussion of relative age in Chapter 4 is both interesting and relevant. Obviously, psychological, social and emotional development will vary between age ranges, but the context of this resource is on the physical aspects of growth, development and maturation. The variable tempo of young people's growth and development will be explained and highlighted throughout. As already touched upon, this variability becomes more acute around puberty, when young people (usually in their early teens) may exhibit a wide range of physiques and developmental differences that need to be considered when planning and implementing programmes. Although this may be more of an issue in sports incorporating a squad system, the individual profiling of young performers to set appropriate programmes is not yet common practice throughout sports coaching.

As an overview, *Coaching the Young Developing Performer* should help coaches to access crucial information, with key messages outlined and then revisited throughout. As with all good coaching practice, repetition is no bad thing.

Outline of Content, Structure and Key Messages

In **Chapter 2**, Craig Williams provides an overview of the issues associated with the different rates of growth, development and maturation of young people. The aim of this chapter is to introduce and clarify the terminology that will be used throughout the resource, and discuss the maturation of different biological systems, not just through chronological age, but also by biological age.

The chapter explains what growth and development entail and why it is important coaches understand the principles and issues relevant to the planning and implementation of programmes for young performers in their development years.

Definitions will be offered so coaches can develop their knowledge. Although coach-friendly language is used throughout, coaches must accept the learning of a common, technical language is necessary to arrive at a common understanding and to avoid miscommunication. Sensitive ethical and child welfare issues are listed and monitoring strategies contributing to a coaching environment safeguarding children are provided.

Basic patterns of existing growth and development as young people move from infancy to adulthood are explained, with relevant implications for coaching programmes set out. Additionally, the main aspects that can be readily observed and

measured are discussed. Explanation is provided as to the importance of observing and measuring these aspects, so a deeper understanding and appreciation is developed. The growth spurt (onset of PHV itself) is introduced as an important concept to help coaches and other support staff plan programmes for individual performers.

In monitoring growth and development, the reasons for, and benefits of, taking measurements of individual young performers over an extended period (longitudinal measurement) are explained. Implications for coaches applying such measurements are given. For example, how procedures can be fitted into programmes, the frequency and timing of measurements, and the fundamental medical issues involved. Of specific interest for coaches who work with mixed sex groups and/or boys and girls separately, is an explanation of the differences in growth, development and monitoring procedures for young males and females. Specific examples are provided and implications for coaching identified.

At the end of this chapter, the different elements of information presented are brought together to help coaches and other support staff to understand aspects of growth, development and maturation that can be monitored and measured. This should assist coaches in assessing each performer as an individual, knowing 'where they are', thus developing a more relevant training and competition schedule. Details of monitoring and measuring are given in Chapter 6.

An important message to take from Chapter 2 is that coaches need to understand every child is developmentally different. Therefore, the need to monitor every young performer's growth and development can easily be understood, individualised programmes can be developed, and the likelihood of young performers achieving their true potential can be increased.

Chapter 3, written by Istvan Balyi and Graham Ross, builds on the concepts of growth, development and maturation, as introduced in Chapter 2, and links them to the key training principles underpinning athletic performance. The principles, processes and issues coaches need to address when planning annual programmes for their young, developing performers are set out. Although based on scientific research, it is important to link them to the empirical evidence and practical experience of coaches working with young developmental performers.

The aim of this chapter is to provide relevant information that increases coaches' understanding of how to develop and produce annual programmes. Scientific principles will be identified and applied to the planning and implementation of actual programmes. A key theme of modern coach education and resources such as this, is that it is not what coaches know which is important, but, rather, what they **do** with their knowledge. This means how they apply it in their coaching behaviour and in the programmes they conduct in their own coaching environment. As outlined earlier, this resource is written for coaches working with young competitive performers, rather than those working at a recreational level. The chapter provides a set of principles and biological markers that provide coaches with the tools to develop individualised programmes for young performers wishing to maximise their sporting potential.

Research into adaptation to training is explained, enabling coaches to link basic principles to the training of young performers. The concept of trainability is then analysed together with an explanation of the sensitive periods of training for different physical and skill capabilities. The importance of **trainability** and

adaptation is discussed, and relevant studies are presented to support and justify the approach to coaching young performers that is being recommended. The concept of training windows has been introduced in *Coaching for Long-term Athlete Development: to improve participation and performance in sport* (Stafford, 2005). If young performers are to be given the best chance of reaching their potential, research indicates these training windows are specific and important times for training different physical and motor skill capabilities. Links are made to the so-called five Ss of training and performance (speed, skill, stamina, suppleness and strength) as set out by former British Athletics Director of Coaching Frank Dick and familiar to many coaches and other support staff. Each of the five are explored in relation to the existing opportunities for the different stages in the growth, development and maturation of an individual young performer.

PHV is explained and a link made to the training windows. Important reference points are identified through the different phases of PHV, with examples and diagrams provided to increase understanding. An obvious area of concern for coaches is when and how to train physical, movement and sport-specific skills, so precise information is given regarding optimal training windows for the five Ss. Reference is made to early and late maturation, but the implications for programme design are identified, in detail, in **Chapter 4**.

Throughout Chapter 4, general and specific guidance and advice on the implications of the information given is provided. The importance of coaches integrating, prioritising and sequencing the training and competition activities their young performers experience in relation to their individual growth and development needs, is discussed in detail.

In Chapters 2 and 3, a number of concepts such as early and late maturation, early and late specialisation and relative age, are raised as factors that will impact on quality training of young performers as individuals.

In Chapter 4, therefore, each of these concepts are discussed in greater detail. The impact each has on the subsequent development and retention of young performers in sport is vital for coaches to understand. How each concept informs the planning and coaching of young performers should be a real, practical consideration, especially for coaches working with young performers from pre-puberty to adulthood.

The phases of growth introduced in Chapter 2 and the sensitive periods of trainability in Chapter 3 are developed in greater depth. In relation to the phases of growth, the relevance of the onset of PHV, and PHV itself, is linked to each of the five Ss of training and performance.

By the end of Chapter 4, key information on growth, development and maturation that coaches need to plan individualised and quality programmes for young, developing performers at different chronological and biological ages, will have been covered. For further help in designing, planning and developing preparation programmes, *Planning and Periodisation* (Pankhurst, 2007) is a useful resource.

Chapter 5 is particularly important as it provides coaches and support staff with applied and practical training and competition plans, for different age groups in two late specialisation sports.

The aim of this chapter is to produce a good practice guide highlighting the common themes and principles that emerge from two different sports. From these two case studies, coaches should be able to extract key information to assist them in their own coaching role within their sport.

The first study, written by Brent Hills, Dawn Scott and Misia Gervis, concerns women's football and, as such, is team based. The second comes from tennis, an individual sport for both males and females, and is written by Anne Pankhurst and Istvan Balyi. Both case studies are used as specific examples of effective programmes and annual plans for young, developing performers (players). They are structured in the same way, both focusing on the specific demands of the sport as a primary consideration. The studies cover the first three stages of the current LTAD model and examine each stage from the viewpoint of the five Ss of training and performance. In addition, a further five factors relating to the different psychological, social and lifestyle issues impacting on training and performance are considered.

Coaches will note that the plans for the two sports, at each stage of LTAD, evidence significant similarities. This is not surprising, bearing in mind that key issues relating to growth and development for the particular age range have been considered in the construction of both programmes. A difference between them is apparent, however, in the specific plans and programmes. Football is a seasonal sport, while tennis is a year-round sport.

Chapter 5 gives key references to help coaches develop their background knowledge, with the case studies illuminating and reinforcing relevant principles. Both highlight the progressive development of programmes to maximise windows of trainability, with key issues and solutions being identified.

Written by Craig Williams, **Chapter 6** takes, as its base, the biological aspects of growth, development and maturation, as examined in Chapter 2 and throughout this resource. It focuses on the measurement protocols and procedures for the effective monitoring of young performers' growth and development. The accurate measurement processes and the relevant tools and equipment needed to monitor growth in terms of stature, sitting height, leg length, arm span and body weight, especially during the onset of PHV, are described in detail. Coaches are then given the means to undertake such measurements if specialist support staff are not readily available. More advanced measurements are also described, although most coaches, for a variety of reasons, will be unlikely to use these in their day-to-day work, unless operating within a well-resourced programme with specialist support staff.

After reading this chapter, coaches should be able to undertake basic, accurate measurements in an appropriate manner, plot growth rates and calculate PHV. However, it is the coach's ability to **apply** the information obtained from measurement protocols that is most important: this is covered in detail. The chapter is also important in giving coaches an understanding of the key strengths and weaknesses of each identified measurement method. Attention is given to other aspects of development that will benefit from measurement, and an assessment is made of how relevant and useful these can be. No coverage of such a topic would be complete without a consideration of the ethical and sensitive nature of the issues involved in monitoring young people's growth and development. Coaches should be aware knowledge and consideration of these issues is fundamental to developing a monitoring environment that is both effective in providing essential information to guide programme planning, and in safeguarding the rights and welfare of young performers at an impressionable and vulnerable stage of their development.

Chapter 7 summarises the main conclusions and recommendations of each preceding chapter, while outlining the next steps. Content and central messages, together with important general and specific guidance and advice, are highlighted. Important issues for governing bodies of sport and coaches are reinforced. Issues that arise from working with different types of information and tracking young performers, as they mature and develop, are provided. Additional sources of information are identified as to where coaches can obtain further help, such as in higher education and other resource bases.

Overall, the purpose of *Coaching the Young Developing Performer* is to give coaches a good understanding of the key content, structure and messages of working with developing performers, in terms of their growth, development and maturation. As stated earlier, LTAD is an evolving framework that is, and should be, subject to continuous scrutiny and improvement. This is much like quality coaching. Coaches should constantly be seeking feedback on the appropriateness and effectiveness of their programmes, their knowledge and their coaching behaviour. Feedback from performers and fellow coaches can be particularly useful in helping evaluate coaching. However, constant learning, self-analysis and reflection are also very important tools. This resource should be read with an open mind. Undoubtedly, some
of the material will cause coaches to question their existing practice. When this does occur, *Coaching the Young Developing Performer* has served a very valuable purpose. The real intention for this resource is to enable coaches to put their developing knowledge and understanding to good use, by practically applying their learning to actual programmes they plan and implement for young performers.

In recent years, coach education has moved away from focusing on the more theoretical aspects. As already acknowledged in this chapter, it is not necessarily the increase in knowledge that will make a difference, but rather what coaches **do** with this knowledge and how they **apply** it. Certainly, key principles and core values must be appreciated and understood, but it is much more important that these are reflected in the practical programmes coaches undertake with their young performers. This will only be achieved if more coaches work with their young performers and others to produce programmes that are truly performer-centred and developmentally appropriate.

Coaching the Young Developing Performer is the first resource of its kind, bringing together a number of contributors to discuss best practice in the training of young, developing performers. It is designed to answer the many questions asked by coaches and other support staff about how to optimise the chances of developing potential in young performers. This intention will be realised when coaches read and engage fully with the material that follows.

References

Hagger, M. (2005) *Coaching Young Performers*. Leeds: Coachwise Business Solutions/The National Coaching Foundation. ISBN: 978-1-902523-56-9.

Pankhurst, A. (2007) *Planning and Periodisation*. Leeds: Coachwise Business Solutions/The National Coaching Foundation. ISBN: 978-1-905540-43-3.

Stafford, I. (2005) *Coaching for Long-term Athlete Development: to improve participation and performance in sport*. Leeds: Coachwise Business Solutions/The National Coaching Foundation. ISBN: 978-1-902523-70-5.

Chapter 2: An Overview of Growth and Development: Peak Height Velocity (PHV)

Craig Williams

Introduction

The purpose of this chapter is to give an overview of the growth, development and maturation of young performers from a coach's perspective. The following information will clarify the terminology required by coaches as they develop their knowledge of the subject area. It will explain the differences between male and female growth patterns, discuss the methods of monitoring growth, development and maturation, and outline some ethical and sensitive issues surrounding monitoring procedures. The reasons why the measurement and monitoring of stature (ie standing height) and, in particular, PHV is so important for coaches, will be discussed. The principles of measurement and how to use the information for planning programmes also form part of the discussion.

When reading the chapter, it is important to place information in the context of certain key issues.

1. Every young person is different and so programmes need to be individualised.

2. The process of monitoring needs to be handled in an ethical and sensitive manner.

3. Coaches need to understand the importance and benefits for young developmental performers of having optimal training, competition and recovery programmes, to ensure their long-term development.

The chapter includes the following sections:

1. Growth – Defining the Key Terms

2. Patterns of Growth

3. Male and Female Growth Patterns: The Differences

4. Methods of Monitoring Growth

5. The Importance and Use of Growth Measurements in Coaching

6. Ethical and Sensitive Issues for Coaches

7. Conclusion.

1. Growth – Defining the Key Terms

To understand the impact of growth, maturation and development when planning coaching programmes for young performers, it is necessary to become familiar with, and understand, the following terms:

• growth, development and maturation (including PHV)

• skeletal maturation

• sexual maturation (including menarche)

• chronological age and biological maturity.

Growth, Development and Maturation (including PHV)

Growth refers to observable and measurable step-by-step changes in an individual. Malina (1984) describes growth as 'measurable changes in body size: for example, height, weight and fatness' (body mass). Growth implies a series of developmental stages that follow the same pattern in everybody. Apart from differences in diet, exercise and health, which, if extreme, may affect these stages, all people will follow a similar growth and maturational pattern.

> Besides infancy, the next and most significant growth pattern is commonly known as the adolescent growth spurt. During this period, individuals experience maximum rate of height growth, referred to as peak height velocity. Growth patterns can provide coaches with vital information about their performers.

Development can be defined as either referring to biological or behavioural development. The former describes the process of differentiation and specialisation of cells into different cell types, tissues and organs, while the latter refers to acquiring social, intellectual and cognitive competences within the context of the emerging personality of the child and the surroundings in which they are brought up (Malina, Bouchard and Bar-Or, 2004). Growth and maturation are synonymous with development.

Maturation is often referred to as progress made towards the biologically mature state and can be defined as 'the timing and tempo (rate) of the biological system as it matures' (Malina and Bouchard, 1991). Another definition, developed by Tihanyi (1990), refers to 'qualitative system changes, both structural and functional in nature, in the organism's progress towards maturity: for example, the change of cartilage to bone in the skeleton'. Maturation differs from growth in that, although biological systems mature at different rates, all individuals reach the same end point and become fully mature. Maturation can vary depending on the biological system (eg skeletal or sexual) being examined. For example, skeletal and sexual maturity may not be progressing at a similar rate. The growth, development and maturation stages (patterns) provide valuable background information for coaches about individual performers.

Skeletal Maturation

Increases in height occur because of growth, especially in long bones. This process continues until the growth plates, usually located at the ends of bones, mature fully. During growth, bone formation exceeds bone-cell absorption and exercises that stress the bone stimulate it to become denser and wider. A skeleton composed of denser, stronger bone is able to withstand stress better.

> The process of skeletal maturation has important ramifications for coaches working with performers whose bones are growing. It follows that during the growth spurt, performers could be prone to overuse injury and, in extreme cases, long-term damage from certain sporting activities. The vulnerability chart in Chapter 3, Appendix 5 is a useful reference.

Examples of overuse injury include:

- the impact on the knee joint when bowling in cricket
- overuse shoulder injuries in swimming and tennis
- wrist injuries in gymnastics.

Sexual Maturation

It is important for coaches to understand the physical and psychological implications of sexual maturation on young performers. Assessment of sexual maturation by coaches is problematic: professional, medical assistance should be sought. Even when this is available, and strict ethical guidelines are followed, it is a particularly sensitive issue. Bearing this in mind, it is perhaps more beneficial for coaches to focus on the process and outcomes of a young performer's sexual maturation, rather than conducting detailed monitoring. The following examples illustrate how process and outcomes could be used.

Marshall (1978) reported on the occurrence of menarche after PHV. Menarche is the onset of the first menstrual cycle. The age when this occurs in girls appears significant. The average time period between PHV and the onset of menarche is about 1.2–1.3 years (Tanner and Davies, 1985). Therefore, with the support and informed consent of the parents and performers concerned, coaches could usefully record when menarche started as evidence of sexual maturation. As menarche occurs late in the pubertal sequence, where growth has not been monitored, the coach can be reasonably sure PHV has occurred because, on average, menarche occurs a little over a year after PHV.

Other indicators have been used to assess sexual maturity, although these are less well researched. They include:

- armpit hair
- facial hair
- voice change.

Armpit hair has previously been rated on a three-point scale of: 1. none present 2. slight growth 3. adult distribution (Billewicz et al, 1981). In girls, armpit hair usually appears after PHV, but before menarche. In boys, it tends to be close to, or just after, PHV.	**Facial hair** in boys is rated on the following four-point scale: 1. none, with downy hair only 2. an increase in length of hair with pigmentation of hair at the corners of the upper lip, spreading medially to complete the moustache 3. appearance of hair on the upper part of the cheeks and in the midline just below the lower lip 4. hair on the sides and lower border of the chin (Billewicz et al, 1981). The development of facial hair in boys (and also voice change) usually appears after PHV.	**Voice change** in boys is noticeable during the adolescent growth spurt and has also been rated on a three-point scale: 1. unbroken (childlike, pre-pubertal) 2. signs of breaking, but not fully broken (ie there is a change in pitch) 3. definitely broken and adult like (Billewicz et al, 1981).

An easier scale could be to use voice change or no voice change. For boys, the voice usually changes fully after PHV, but initial change varies across the age range.

As with other maturity indicators already discussed, armpit hair, facial hair and voice change are all continuous processes with overlapping stages. These three indicators occur rather late in the maturational cycle, so are not so useful as indicators of sexual maturation.

> As young performers progress through puberty, both physical and psychological changes will become apparent and coaches must be sensitive to all such changes. Careful observation of growth patterns and behaviour is something that will help all coaches develop appropriately sensitive and individual training programmes.

Chronological Age and Biological Maturity

Chronological age refers to the actual number of years and days elapsed since birth. It refers, therefore, to the measurable period of time elapsed since the birth date (the date on the birth certificate). **Biological maturity**, however, refers to the physiological age of the individual. This may not be the same as the chronological age, as it depends on the rate of growth: for example, of the skeleton or sexual organs. Biological maturity can vary greatly between individuals, independently of chronological age. Measures to assess biological maturity are often plotted against chronological age to establish, what is often referred to in literature, as biological or developmental age. In Section 4 of this chapter and in Chapter 3, the importance of the differences between chronological age and biological or developmental age will become apparent.

> It is essential for coaches to appreciate and understand the differences between chronological and biological age, because they have significant implications for planning programmes and coaching sport with young developing performers. A number of other terms such as 'sensitive periods of trainability', 'windows of opportunity', 'readiness' (see Chapter 3), 'early and late maturity', the concepts of 'early and late specialisation' and 'relative age effect' (see Chapter 4) are important for coaches to understand, because successful planning and coaching for young performers will impact upon performance.

2. Patterns of Growth

As outlined in the previous section on growth and maturation, people tend to follow a similar pattern of development. This pattern can be divided into four stages:

- Infancy
- Early and middle childhood
- Adolescence
- Adulthood.

In this resource, where PHV is being used for monitoring and charting growth, the following general patterns will be distinguished for all children (see Figure 1):

1. a rapid gain in infancy up to one year old (infancy is defined from birth to one year)

2. a deceleration of growth in early childhood (1–6 years of age)

3. a steady rate during middle childhood (6–12 years of age)

4. a rapid growth during the growth spurt (onset of PHV) (12–14 years of age)

5. a slow increase until growth ceases, with the attainment of adulthood.

More detailed information on the phases of growth can be found in Chapter 4.

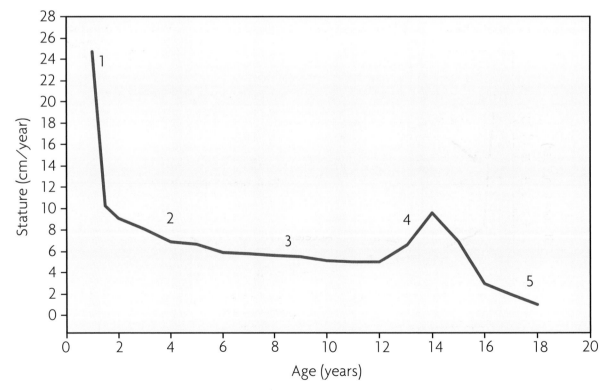

Figure 1: A typical velocity growth curve for an individual moving from infancy to adulthood

Infancy

Post-natal growth consists of three periods (infancy, childhood [early and middle] and adolescence). Infancy comprises the first year of life and is accompanied by a rapid increase in body size and neuromuscular coordination. The increase in stature for a one year old can be up to 25cm in one year.

Early and Middle Childhood

After infancy, and for the next year, the increase in stature is about 12.5cm – half of the above figure. The next period follows on from early childhood (two years plus) through to adolescence and is characterised by a steady increase in growth (on average 5–6cm per year) and maturation, with large increases in motor coordination.

> Coaches, teachers and parents should encourage the development of motor skills, FUNdamentals, movement skills and basic sport skills during this stage.

Adolescence

This is the most important stage from a coaching perspective because of individual rapid growth. There are two important time periods within adolescence. The first involves the onset of the adolescent growth spurt, which is defined by rapid growth in height and weight. This is also known as puberty, when the sex organs become fully developed.

> The adolescent stage is sometimes judged, therefore, as sexual maturation. It is partly for this reason that adolescence is so difficult to define in terms of assessing the beginning and end of this stage.

The second period concerns when the highest growth rate (PHV) is reached, after which it begins decelerating. This remains an important part of adolescence, as it is often the time of other bodily changes such as increases in trunk length, strength and body mass (Ackland and Bloomfield, 1996). The time post-PHV also has implications for coaches. Adolescent performers may appear rather awkward, clumsy and uncoordinated at this time and may need help adjusting to their rapidly changing body proportions.

Adulthood

In adulthood, growth in terms of stature begins to plateau and eventually cease. Most published studies show growth finishing around 18 to 19 years of age. However, it is important for coaches to understand it is not uncommon for some men and women to experience growth in stature of up to several centimetres per year into their early twenties. Clearly, individual timing (when growth does end) and tempo (rate of deceleration of growth) can be different for each person. Coaches working with young performers in the 18–23 age range will notice quite striking changes in physique during this period, especially when effective conditioning programmes are being undertaken.

A velocity curve showing the five main stages of growth, from infancy to early adulthood, is shown in Figure 2. A number of growth-related terms are shown, such as decelerating growth, onset of the adolescent growth spurt and PHV. The decelerating part of the growth curve shows when growth is declining from one year to the next. The onset of the adolescent growth curve is taken to be the initiation of the pubertal growth spurt that rapidly translates into an accelerating upwards slope of the curve. Eventually, the highest rate of growth achieved in any one particular year (cm/y) is defined as the point of PHV. After PHV, the growth rate decelerates until stature growth ceases in adulthood.

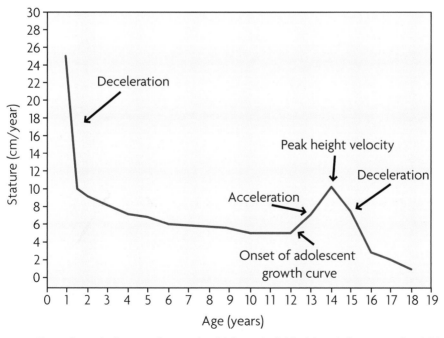

Figure 2: A velocity growth curve (cm/y) for an individual from infancy to early adulthood.

A more detailed graph of the stages of growth is given in Figure 16, Chapter 4.

Key Concepts and Summary

Growth and Patterns of Growth

The need for coaches to understand the process of measuring the growth of young performers to identify and understand key growth patterns is vital. This will enable training programmes to be adjusted for the individual, to ensure optimal training effect both in the short and long term. Graphs similar to Figure 2 are commonly used to plot, monitor and assess individual growth patterns.

- The timing and rate of growth are unique to each child. Although the pattern will be similar, no two children will experience the same growth rate or timing of growth.

- Stature and the recording of the start of menarche in girls are common indicators (or biological markers) of growth and maturation.

- Most girls experience menarche approximately a year after PHV.

- Armpit hair in boys and girls and voice change and facial hair in boys have been used as indicators of secondary sexual characteristics. However, they are crude indicators, as they tend to occur late in the sequential changes during puberty.

3. Male and Female Growth Patterns: The Differences

Peak Height Velocity

The growth velocity curve in Figure 3 shows the differences between gender. Girls typically experience growth spurt up to two years earlier than boys. The growth spurt of boys, while lasting up to two years longer, results in them catching and overtaking girls in terms of stature. Timescales can, however, change slightly when measuring different ethnic groups. Additionally, on average, males tend to be taller and heavier than females, partly as a consequence of up to two years' additional growing time.

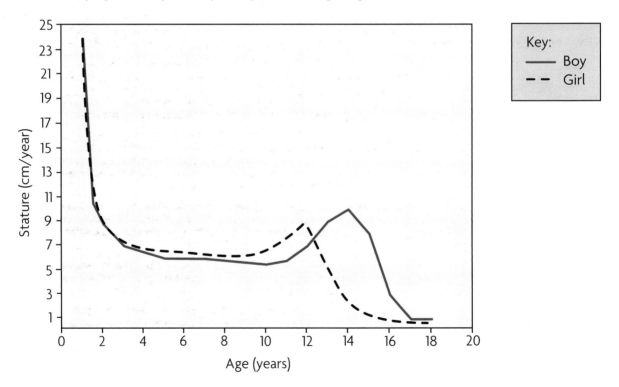

Figure 3: A simple growth curve for one boy and one girl (stature measures taken once a year)

The following key points should be noted by coaches:

- It is usual for the onset of the adolescent growth spurt in the UK to occur between 8.5 and 10.5 years of age in girls, and between 10.3 and 12.1 years in boys.

- The earlier the growth spurt starts, the more intense the rate of growth.

- Boys who are early maturers tend to be more muscular, have shorter legs and broader hips. Girls who mature early have shorter legs and narrower shoulders than their late maturing counterparts.

- On average, the total growth in the year before PHV for girls is about 7.5/8cm (three inches) and 9/9.5cm (3.7 inches) for boys.

- The age that PHV is reached ranges between 10–12 years for girls and 13.5–14.5 years for boys.

- Different growth studies will give varying mean values, but the above ranges are typically found throughout Western countries.

(Freeman et al., 1995; Tanner et al., 1966a,b; Tanner et al., 1985).

The adolescent growth spurt has significant implications for both boys' and girls' performance in sport. The two to three years' advantage girls possessed in terms of strength, stature and body mass begins to level off as growth rates decelerate. Boys then begin to make improvement in terms of strength, speed, power and motor skills, and gradually overtake girls. The implication of these growth and maturation stages means different time periods for girls and boys should be used to develop different skills such as speed, motor skills, endurance, strength and power.

Peak Weight Velocity

If body weight is measured using a similar method to stature, curves can be plotted to define the peak weight velocity (PWV). This is the highest rate of growth in weight (kg/year) experienced by the performer in any one particular year. Typically, in boys, the maximum increase in weight is about 0.2–0.4kg a year after PHV. For girls, the maximum increase in weight is about 0.3–0.9kg a year after PHV. A significant proportion of weight change is due to muscle, which accounts for the largest tissue mass, and is also the most metabolically active system in the human body. Despite this, skeletal muscle has not been extensively investigated in children (Eriksson, 1972; Bell et al, 1980; Berg et al, 1986). This has largely been as a result of the invasive nature into the study of muscle performance.

Muscle mass increases with age and, although boys have slightly higher muscle mass than girls from six years onwards, the larger gender differences only begin to emerge during and after puberty. Between the ages of 5–17, muscle mass as a percentage of body mass in boys increases from approximately 42% to 54%. In girls, the increase is both less and at an earlier age, from 40% to 45% between the ages of 5–13. In both sexes, muscle mass percentage then stabilises. After the age of 13, increases in fat accumulation in girls results in the relative increase in body mass being accounted for by fat. Consequently, for girls, the contribution of muscle mass to body mass declines.

In general, strength increases linearly with age in both boys and girls, with an acceleration for both genders during the adolescent growth spurt. However, the growth spurt for strength in girls is less intense compared to that for boys. When assessing strength and motor performance, it is important other factors such as body size, physique and body composition are considered. There is great variation in strength and motor performance between young performers, which cannot be explained by growth and maturational factors. It can, however, be explained by motivation, practice and training, learning and environmental factors.

Estimates of fat-free mass show a growth curve similar to those of stature and body mass. During adolescence, sex differences become established. Female adult values for fat-free mass are attained earlier than males. During the adolescent growth spurt, girls' body fat percentage increases to about 25% of body mass (an increase from 18% during childhood). In boys, this declines to approximately 12%–14% of body mass (a decrease from about 16% during childhood).

One of the key implications of these physiological differences is the advantage males gain in muscle strength and power, especially around the shoulders, which can have a significant effect on training and sporting performance. The issues relating to optimal times to develop strength for performers are examined in more detail in the next chapter.

The theoretical model overleaf (Figure 4) highlights the fact that, while pre-pubertal children have been found to increase the actual size of their muscles (hypertrophy), the majority of strength gains, prior to the growth spurt, are explained by improved motor skill coordination, increased activation of the muscles and other neural effects. After the growth spurt, when gender differences in strength begin to increase rapidly, the effects of hormones (eg testosterone) and muscle fibre maturation are thought to explain reported improvements in strength.

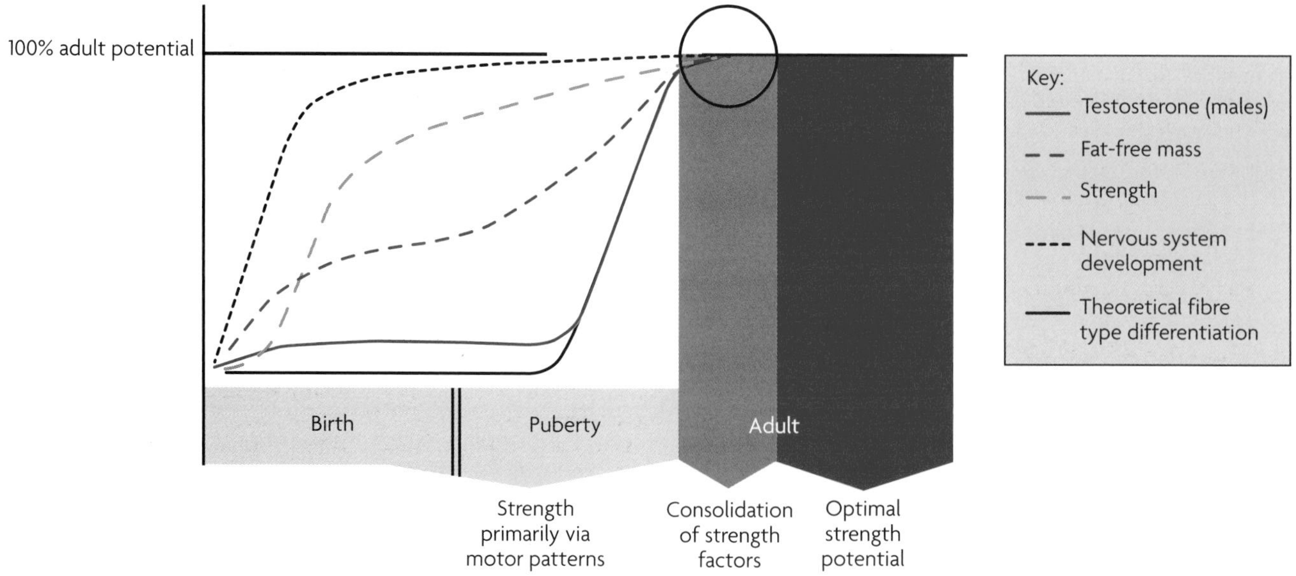

Figure 4: A theoretical model integrating a number of developmental factors related to muscle strength adaptations from birth to adulthood

Key Concepts and Summary

Male and Female Differences

Coaches must understand the different patterns of growth and development between boys and girls to ensure they can identify and relate these to their own performers. This would enable adjustments to guarantee an optimal training programme is established, both in the short and long term. Adjustments to the training programme are considered in the next chapter.

- Girls experience the onset of growth spurt approximately two years before boys (at around 8.5–10.5 years of age).

- Boys subsequently catch and overtake girls in terms of growth and maturation.

- This difference between girls and boys has significant implications for the performance of both sexes in sport. Coaches need to be aware of these when designing training and competition programmes.

- The average age PHV is reached ranges between 10–12 years for girls and 13.5–14.5 years for boys (Freeman et al., 1995; Tanner et al., 1966a,b; Tanner et al., 1985).

- PHV has important implications for coaches in terms of the prioritisation of different performance capabilities (eg speed, skills, endurance and strength).

- Muscle mass and body fat changes are the most important factors impacting on performance during adolescence.

- Studies offer average scores and chronological ages. Therefore, it is important to monitor individual growth information and trends.

4. Methods of Monitoring Growth

Kinanthropometry concerns the structure and function of the human body, combining anatomy and physiology. It is used to evaluate human size, shape, proportion, composition, maturation and gross function in relation to exercise and performance (Ross and Marfell-Jones, 1991 in MacDougall, Wenger and Green, 1991). In this section, the methods and techniques used to measure different factors of growth and development are discussed. These are:

- growth and maturation
- skeletal maturation
- sexual maturation
- other biological markers.

Growth and Maturation

Growth and maturation rates are biological processes that should be viewed as connected components. As discussed earlier, a measure frequently used for tracking growth and maturation is **chronological** age. However, the weakness of this measure is that children who are 12 years old on a certain date may be chronologically the same age, but some will be **biologically** more mature than others (see Chronological Age and Biological Maturity earlier in this chapter and the case study on pages 39–41). Those more biologically advanced differ in physique, body composition and often physical performance (Malina, 1984). Biological maturity plays an important role in the development of sports performance, so techniques used to assess maturity need to be understood by coaches (see Chapter 4).

Skeletal Maturation

The most common technique for skeletal assessment is an X-ray, which is usually taken of the hand. However, there are concerns as to how representative the hand is of the whole skeleton (see Chapter 6). In one study (Roche, 1976), X-rays of the hand and knee varied by one or more years in some children. This form of measurement may be hazardous to children and is not commonly utilised in sports performance. Non-invasive instruments such as magnetic resonance imaging (MRI) and magnetic resonance spectroscopy (MRS) have largely superseded the X-ray, though usually only for research purposes.

Another valid technique is to measure body size or segments of the body (see Chapter 6). Somatic maturity is often used in association with the age of PHV and PWV. The method of analysis requires data to be collected over many years and is inappropriate for short-term studies, though it can easily be implemented by coaches.

Sexual Maturation

The predominant assessment of sexual maturation is Tanner's stages of pubic hair, breast and genitalia development (Tanner, 1962). The initiation of secondary sex characteristics is sub-divided into five categories. Stage 1 indicates the pre-pubertal state, signifying a lack of sexual development, while Stage 2 shows an initial progression of each characteristic. Research in America and Europe suggests Tanner's Stage 2 occurs between 10.6 and 11.4 years for girls and 11.0 and 12.0 years for boys (Malina, 1978; Malina, Bouchard and Bar-Or, 2004).

Stages 3 and 4 represent continued maturation of the breast, genitalia and pubic hair. These stages also represent a difficult period in which to differentiate the maturational process. Stage 5 indicates adult or mature development of each characteristic.

Although the age at which these stages are attained is variable, trends in several studies show most boys are at Stages 3 and 4 at the time of PHV, while the majority of girls tend to be at Stages 2 and 3 at this time.

Tanner's assessment technique for evaluating sexual maturity does have its drawbacks. Firstly, a nurse or doctor is required for examination. This procedure obviously requires an invasion of the performer's privacy, which may be of some concern to adolescents and parents. However, if conducted in a professional and appropriate environment, the level of embarrassment can be significantly reduced. Secondly, for consistency, the same nurse or doctor should, where possible, evaluate all subjects. The subject may be at Stage 1 for pubic hair, but at Stage 2 for breast development. Current evidence suggests there is no consistent relationship between the age at which secondary characteristics develop and the rate of progress through Stages 1–5. In the Harpenden Growth Study (Tanner et al, 1985), some boys passed through the genitalia 2 to genitalia 5 stages in two years, while, for others, it took as long as five years. It is important to remember the development of sexual maturity is a continuous process, upon which there are specific end stages. The implementation of Tanner's assessment technique is most often used in cross-sectional studies. It will, therefore, have a limited applicability to surveys of growth and maturation.

Other Biological Markers

Age at menarche is another commonly reported characteristic of maturity. Menarche tends to occur rather late in the maturational process, often at Stage 4. Marshall (1978) reported the occurrence of menarche after PHV. The mean age difference between PHV and the onset of menarche is about 1.2–1.3 years (see earlier in this chapter) (Tanner and Davies, 1985). If PHV has not been monitored, a simple solution for coaches would be to record when menarche has started for their female performers, because they can then be reasonably sure PHV has occurred. Menarche is usually identifiable by females, so is relatively easy to record.

PHV, or age at PHV, is one of the most commonly recorded variables and is a valid marker of maximum growth rate during childhood and adolescence. The monitoring of growth rate per year can also be used as an indicator for increases in other body segments (eg leg length and trunk length).

Key Concepts and Summary

Monitoring Growth

Different methods can be used to monitor factors of growth and development. Many of the ones outlined may not be suitable or appropriate for a coach to implement without the input of medical staff. These include X-rays and Tanner's assessment technique. However, there are a number of biological markers coaches can use to assess individual stage of growth and development.

- Each method used to measure and monitor growth and maturation has strengths and weaknesses. The method of choice will be determined by access to suitable facilities, equipment and medical staff.

- Chronological age is not necessarily an indicator of biological maturity.

- The procedure for measuring height and weight can be used to give an estimate of the process of maturation. In particular, when measurements of the trends with regards PHV are made, coaches can estimate the stage of maturation and can adjust training programmes accordingly to optimise performer development. (How these training programmes can be adjusted is discussed in Chapter 4.)

- Measurements of growth are perhaps the easiest to take and are within the technical capabilities of most coaches and support teams. In addition, coaches can use information, such as the onset of menarche, to understand where a female performer is in relation to PHV.

- There are many sensitive issues involved when measuring and observing growth and development patterns of performers. If explained sensitively and discretely, the coach can help performers understand their growth and development patterns, both in terms of health education and sport.

5. The Importance and Use of Growth Measurements in Coaching

Close monitoring of growth enables sports scientists and coaches to identify structural (anatomical) or physiological characteristics of performers, which can help plan more appropriate training programmes based on biological age. The previous section discussed methods of measuring growth in young performers, which links to the information given on growth, development and maturation in 'Growth – Defining the Key Terms'. While measurements can be taken for growth, it is clear young performers mature at different rates and times. The fact most girls reach PHV sometime between 10 and 12 years of age and most boys between the ages of 13.5 and 14.5 means it is essential to understand the developmental age, as well as the chronological age, of all young performers. Clearly, there will be some young performers outside these average figures, resulting in the following classifications: early, average and late maturers (see Chapter 4).

> Coaches need to monitor growth in order to adjust training programmes to meet the individual needs of their performers.

Characteristics that help indicate biological maturity are both structural (anatomical) and physiological. The timing and rate of increase in stature are indications of the onset and peak of PHV. During this time, different body segments such as limb length and trunk size change. These changes may or may not be a measure of adult development. There are also differences between boys and girls. Physiological changes affect physical abilities and, thus, physical performance. During adolescence, coaches should be aware of the difficulties of knowing whether improvements in performance are the result of growth and maturation, of early or late maturity, or of training.

It is important coaches monitor the aspects of growth, development and maturation outlined in this chapter. They also need to know when to monitor, as identified below:

- Measurements taken only once will be of limited value, since growth rates are neither linear nor predictable.

- Measurement and monitoring should be a continuous process to be of practical use (see Chapter 6).

- Structured, systematic and longitudinal measurements and monitoring are far more likely to yield reliable and useful information, which can contribute to planning high-quality training programmes.

> A recommended frequency of measurement of stature is once every three months. If this is impractical, every six months would be the recommended minimum.

The use of information derived in the manner recommended can be of great help in matching programmes to the individual performer's stage of development.

The decision regarding which measurements to obtain will be based on the facilities available, the availability of personnel to assist with the process, the impact testing will have on other training activities and the number of children to be measured. It is not worth taking measurements more than four times a year, as the error of measurement is likely to be larger than the increase in growth of the child. (Chapter 6 explains more about the timings of measurements and the technical details of how and when to measure stature.)

A number of sports now utilise the anatomical and physiological characteristics of young performers for talent identification (Bompa, 1985) or talent detection (Russell, 1989). While it is well known specific body types and body segment patterns give adult performers in certain sports a natural advantage (eg being tall in basketball, having short legs and a low centre of gravity in weightlifting, gymnastics and wrestling), the coach's responsibility is to help young performers develop specific skills for their sport at the right time: this can be helped by monitoring growth and development patterns.

Key Concepts and Summary

The Importance and Use of Growth Measurements in Coaching

Performers need to be monitored individually so their programmes of training and competition can be linked to their developmental age and best interests in the long term.

- Measuring and monitoring growth and maturation should be undertaken in a systematic and structured manner, and on a longitudinal basis, to be of value.

- As a consequence of information obtained from a more systematic monitoring system, coaches are able to adapt the volume and priority of training programmes for their young developing performers. This can be done by increasing or decreasing training volume and/or focusing training phases on prioritising speed/skills or endurance/strength.

- Different parts of the body grow and mature at different rates. The timing and tempo of changes in relative size and in the mass of different body segments will be different for every child as they progress through childhood and adolescence to adulthood.

- Coaches need to appreciate that a particular limb length may or may not remain stable throughout the adolescent growth period. The identification of a particular characteristic (physical or physiological) in a pre-adolescent child does not guarantee it will remain so during adolescence and into adulthood.

---

6. Ethical and Sensitive Issues for Coaches

The measurement and monitoring of body size, composition and shape of children is a sensitive issue. Much media publicity has been given to safeguarding children and young people. For all coaches working with children and young people, it is imperative best practice is followed. The Child Protection in Sport Unit (CPSU) has published the *Standards for Safeguarding and Protecting Children in Sport*, which sets out a framework to provide a benchmark to help those involved in sport make informed decisions, and to promote good practice and challenge practice that is harmful to children. This document relates to safeguarding and protecting children, not just for the welfare of each child, but also for the protection of the coach's and officials' integrity from unwarranted or malicious accusations.

The practicalities of measuring children's growth means sports clothing may be minimal and measurement may be conducted in changing rooms. Therefore, potential problems can easily arise. It is imperative each coach and support team follows clear guidelines to minimise such problems. If at any time the child feels uncomfortable, alternative arrangements should be discussed, such as having a parent take the measurements at home. Please see 'Club Guidelines' on the CPSU website (www.thecpsu.org.uk) for further guidance.

Developmentally, adolescence is a time of many anthropometric, physiological and psychological changes in boys and girls, resulting in great concern for body image. Ideally, measurement of body size or composition would be conducted by same gender teams. Failing this, it is next best practice to have at least one same gender person as the children being tested. Same gender testing teams opposite to the gender of the child participants are not recommended. In squads that cater for both sexes, it is good practice if boys and girls are tested separately.

Key Concepts and Summary

Ethical and Sensitive Issues for Coaches

This section has examined the key ethical and sensitive issues coaches need to be aware of when measuring and monitoring the growth patterns of performers.

- All coaches should be aware of the regulations and recommendations for safeguarding and protecting children, together with best practice information for themselves and their support teams.

- It is recommended a minimum of two adults are present and that those conducting the measurements are the same gender as the young performers being measured. If this is not possible, at least one member of the team should be of the same gender as the performers being measured.

- Body image is an important concept during the adolescent years. Therefore, the coach should be sensitive to the individual when focusing on measurements that monitor this aspect.

7. Conclusion

Coaches working with young developmental performers need to understand the information in this chapter to use the indicators of growth and maturation, monitoring of stature and other body segment measures, wherever possible. The easiest strategy is to make measurement an integral part of ongoing testing (eg performance profiling), or part of a medical check-up completed on an annual or more frequent basis. It is also recommended coaches and support teams begin to rationalise their approaches to training, based on the measured and monitored growth patterns and estimated maturity status of individual young performers. By implementing these simple procedures, coaches will be able to plan and adjust the training, competition and recovery programme according to the individual growth and maturation rates of each young developing performer.

References

Ackland, T.R. and Bloomfield, J. (1996) 'Stability of human proportions through adolescent growth', *The Australian Journal of Science and Medicine in Sport*, 28 (2): 57–60.

Bell, R.D., MacDougall, J.D., Billeter, R. and Howard, H. (1980) 'Muscle fibre types and morphometric analysis of skeletal muscle in six-year-old children', *Medicine and Science in Sports and Exercise*, 12: 28–31.

Berg, A., Kim, S.S. and Keul, J. (1986) 'Skeletal muscle enzyme activities in healthy young subjects', *International Journal of Sports Medicine*, 7: 236–239.

Billewicz, W.Z., Fellowes, H.M. and Thomson A.M. (1981) 'Pubertal changes in boys and girls in Newcastle-upon-Tyne', *Annals of Human Biology*, 8: 211–219.

Bompa T. (1985) 'Talent identification', *Sports Science Periodical on Research and Technology in Sport*, GN-1, February: 1–11.

Eriksson, B.O. (1972) 'Physical training, oxygen supply and muscle metabolism in 11-13-year-old boys', *Acta Physiologica Scandinavica*, 384 (Suppl. 1): 1–48.

Freeman, J.V., Cole, T.J., Chinn, S., Jones, P.R.M., White, E.M., Preece, M.A. (1995) 'Cross-sectional stature and weight reference curves for the UK 1990,' *Archives of Disease in Childhood*, 73: 17–24.

Kramer, W.J. and Fleck, S.J. (1993) *Strength training for young performers*. Champaign, Illinois: Human Kinetics. ISBN: 0-873223-96-9.

Malina, R.M., Bouchard, C. and Bar-Or, O. (2004) *Growth, Maturation and Physical Activity*. Champaign, Illinois: Human Kinetics. ISBN: 978-0-880118-82-8.

Malina, R.M. and Bouchard, C. (1991) *Growth, Maturation and Physical Activity*. Champaign, Illinois: Human Kinetics. ISBN: 0-873223-21-7.

Malina, R.M. (1984) 'Physical Growth and Maturation', in Thomas, J.R. (ed.) *Motor Development During Childhood and Adolescence*. Minneapolis: Burgess International Group. ISBN: 978-0-024202-01-7. 2–26.

Malina, R.M. (1978) 'Adolescent growth and maturation: selected aspects of current research', *Yearbook of Physical Anthropology*, 21: 63–94.

Marshall, W.A. (1978) 'Puberty', in Faulkner, F. and Tanner, J.M. (eds) *Human Growth*, Volume 2: Post-natal growth. New York: Plenum: 141–181.

Roche, A.F. (1976) *Skeletal Maturity: The Knee Joint As a Biological Indicator*. New York: Springer. ISBN: 978-0-306309-00-7.

Ross, W.D. and Marfell-Jones, M.J. (1991) 'Kinanthropometry,' in MacDougall, J.D, Wenger, H.A. and Green, H.J. (eds) (1991) *Physiological testing of the High Performance Athlete* (2nd edition). Champaign, Illinois: Human Kinetics. ISBN: 978-0-873223-00-3.

Russell, K. (1989) 'Athletic talent: from detection to perfection', *Sports Science Periodical on Research and Technology in Sport*, GY-I, January: 1–7.

Tanner, J.M. and Davies, P.S.W. (1985) 'Clinical longitudinal standards for height and height velocity for North American children', *Journal of Pediatrics*, 107: 317–329.

Tanner J., Whitehouse, R. and Takaishi, M. (1966a) 'Standards from birth to maturity for height, weight, height velocity and weight velocity: British children 1965 Part I,' *Archives of Disease in Childhood*, 41: 457–471.

Tanner J., Whitehouse, R., Takaishi, M. (1966b) 'Standards from birth to maturity for height, weight, height velocity and weight velocity: British children 1965 Part II,' *Archives of Disease in Childhood*, 41: 613–635.

Tanner, J.M. (1962) *Growth at Adolescence* (2nd edition), Oxford: Blackwell Scientific Publications. ASIN: B0018DQTBM.

Further Reading

Armstrong N. and Van Mechelen, W. (2008) *Paediatric Exercise Science and Medicine* (2nd edition). Oxford: Oxford University Press. ISBN: 978-0-199232-48-2.

Bar-Or, O. (ed) (1996) *The Child and Adolescent Performer*. London: Blackwell, Scientific Publications. ISBN: 0-865429-04-9.

Maffulli, N., King, J. B., and Helms, P. (1994) 'Training in elite young performers (the training of young performers [TOYA] study): injuries, flexibility and isometric strength', *British Journal of Sports Medicine*, 28 (2): 123–136.

Philippaerts, R.M., Vaeyens, R., Janssens, M., Van Renterghem, B., Matthys, D., Craen, R., Bourgois, J., Vrijens, J., Beunen, G and Malina, R.M. (2006) 'The relationship between peak height velocity and physical performance in youth soccer players', *Journal of Sports Sciences*, 24 (3): 221–230.

Tihanyi, J. (1990) *Long-term Planning for Young Performers: An Overview of the Influences of Growth, Maturation and Development*. Sudbury: Laurentian University.

Williams, C. A. (2007) 'Physiological changes of the young athlete and the effects on sports performance', *SportsEx Medicine*: 6–11.

Chapter 3: Optimal Trainability for the Young Developing Performer

Istvan Balyi and Graham Ross

Introduction

In this chapter, the application and interpretation of a number of scientific principles are combined with the practical experience and findings of leading coaches in sport. Much of the information is supported by coaching and exercise science literature.

The chapter develops the scientific background information previously provided and addresses the specific issues faced by coaches, when planning annual programmes for young developing performers. The objective is to provide key information to increase coaches' understanding of how to develop annual training, competition and recovery programmes to ensure both short- and long-term optimal performance and progression. More specifically, there will be a provision of guidance on how to train performers during:

- childhood – the **FUNdamental stage** (approximate age: 6–8 for females and 6–9 for males)

- pre-puberty – the **Learning to Play and Practice stage** (previously known as the Learning to Train Stage) (approximate age: 8–11 for females and 9–12 for males)

- puberty and post-puberty – the **Training to Train stage** (approximate age: 11–15 for females and 12–16 for males).

The stages given above are part of the long-term athlete development (LTAD) pathway. More detailed information regarding the stages of LTAD can be found in *Coaching for Long-term Athlete Development* (Stafford, 2005, pages 22–23).

This chapter is sectioned as follows:

1. An Overview of Adaptation and Trainability

2. Windows of Trainability

3. Trainability of the Aerobic System (Stamina or Endurance)

4. Trainability of Strength

5. Trainability of Speed

6. Trainability of Movement and Sports Skill

7. Trainability of Suppleness (Flexibility)

8. Summary of Trainability

9. Conclusion.

1. An Overview of Adaptation and Trainability

For the objective of this chapter to be achieved, it is important a number of issues are clarified.

The principles of adaptation and trainability are key to the understanding of growth, development and maturation in sport. It is not the intention, here, to give a comprehensive review of adaptation and trainability literature, but, rather, to generalise and synthesise relevant trends in the literature to guide coaches on how to coach young developing performers. The focus will be on trainability and the importance of understanding its consequences, to best design training programmes for young developing performers. (Note: By doing this, we are highlighting issues that are not utilised, or are poorly utilised, in present coaching practice.)

The terms adaptation and trainability are often used interchangeably in coaching. However, the difference between them is significant. Back in 1930, Harris et al, provided a 'road map', by describing the processes of general, neural and genital development. Such processes should be considered to help understand trainability in young performers.

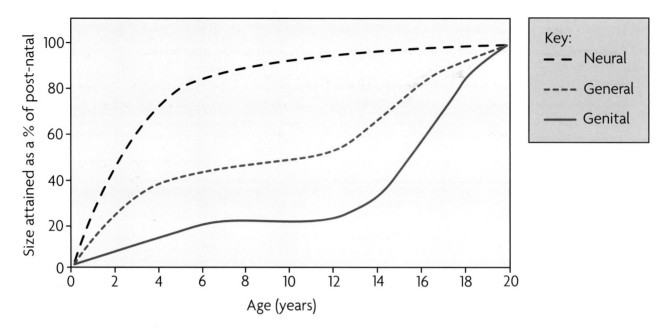

**Figure 5: The influence of maturation in general, neural and genital development up to 20 years of age
(Norris and Smith, 2002, modified from Scammon, 1930)**

Figure 5 Explained

General curve – This describes the growth of the body in terms of stature and weight. It includes the growth patterns of different systems of the body, such as muscle mass, the skeleton, lungs and the heart. The shape of the curve indicates slow but steady development of the body structure/stature between the ages of five and 10–12 years. In simple terms, this gives the opportunity for skill development at this time. During and after puberty, fitness can be exploited because of maturation of the skeletal structures, muscle mass, lungs and the cardiovascular system.

Neural curve – This describes the growth of the brain and the nervous system. Of the central nervous system, 95% is developed by about seven years of age. The shape of the curve suggests early development of the nervous system will give children the opportunity to develop the movement skills of agility, balance, coordination and speed at an early training age. FUNdamental movement and FUNdamental sports skills can, and should, be developed during childhood.

Genital curve – This shows the patterns of growth of both the primary and secondary sex characteristics. Genital tissue shows slow growth, with a latent period during childhood, before extremely rapid growth and maturation during the adolescent growth spurt. The shape of this curve indicates hormonal maturation, which will have a significant contribution to fitness development and performance improvement.

Adaptation

In scientific literature, adaptation refers to alterations that induce functional and/or morphological changes in the body, as a result of a stimulus. The degree of adaptation is dependent on the genetic endowment of the individual. However, the general trends or patterns of individual adaptation can be identified by physiological research. Guidelines are available that clearly delineate the adaptation processes of different systems. For example, adaptation to aerobic endurance, muscular endurance or maximum strength.

Reviewing scientific literature on adaptation to training, Viru and Viru (1993) described the two main influences of training as:

- the action on the muscle myofibrils, induced by resistance or weight training
- the action on the muscle mitochondria, induced by endurance training.

Between these two main influences lie power, sprint and anaerobic interval training.

Nadori (1985) described the adaptation processes as follows (see Figure 6):

1. After the external training load has taken place, changes will occur in the internal milieu of the organism. (The training load is a combination of volume and intensity of training.)

   The changes are:

   – physiological – increased metabolism, increased heart rate and breathing frequency, fluid shifts, increased specific proteins and hormonal changes

   – biochemical – blood lactate, testosterone cortisol ratios, haemoglobin

   – psychological – fatigue, lethargy, lack of concentration, lack of coping.

2. The volume and intensity of the external training load will determine the level of induced fatigue when exercise ceases.

3. The level of induced fatigue will determine the length of the recovery period.

4. If the recovery phase between the two external training loads is too short, under-recovery, overreaching or overtraining can occur in the longer term.

5. If the recovery phase between the two external training loads is too long, the training effect or overcompensation will diminish.

6. Adaptation will be enhanced when the next external training load is introduced, when the organism is in the overcompensation state.

With proper monitoring and sequencing of training activities, adaptation can be enhanced.

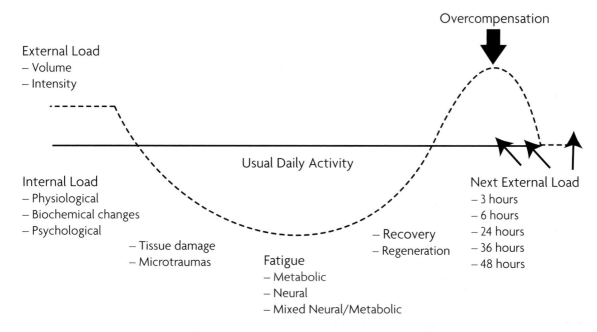

Figure 6: Adaptation to training (Nadori, 1985)

Figure 7 below illustrates and contrasts optimal training, overreach and overtraining. It shows how lack of recovery can lead to overtraining and burnout.

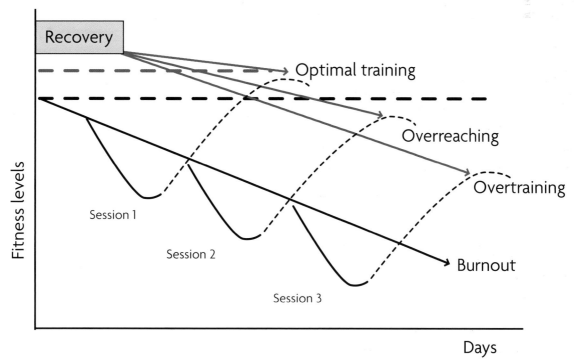

Figure 7: The schema of optimal training, overreaching and overtraining (adapted from McCaffrey, 2004 in Ulster Council, 2006)

Trainability

Bearing in mind the adjacent statement, it is clear critical or sensitive periods for training different skills exist as the individual matures (see Figure 8).

According to Tanner (1989), these periods, in the physiological sense, are ones of increasing sensitivity of a receptor to a highly specific stimulus, followed by decreasing sensitivity and, eventually, a complete lack of response.

A critical or sensitive period of development refers to the point when, in the development of a specific capability, training has optimal effect.

Current scientific insights indicate there are sensitive periods or broad time frames when individuals can learn new tasks efficiently and effectively (Gallahue and Ozmun, 2006). Such periods need to take account of individual differences. For example, whether a performer is an early or late maturer. For the purposes of this chapter, the following definition applies:

> Trainability is defined as the responsiveness of developing individuals to the training stimulus, at different stages of growth and maturation (Malina and Bouchard, 1991).

Windows of trainability refers to the sensitive periods of accelerated adaptation to training, which occur prior to, and during, puberty and early post-puberty. The window is fully open during the sensitive periods of accelerated adaptation to training, and partially open outside of these periods.

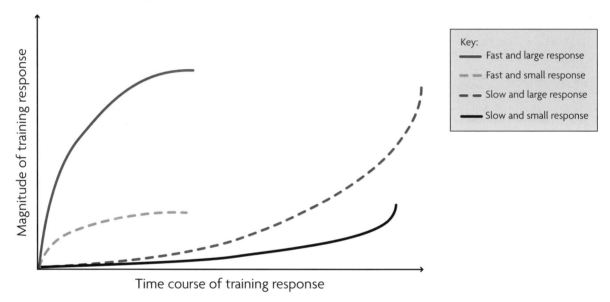

Figure 8: Variation in trainability (adapted from Bouchard et al, 1997 in Canadian Sport for Life, 2009)

The concept of different levels and timescales for individuals to respond to training is one already familiar to coaches.

Figure 8 illustrates a high degree of variation in the trainability of humans, both from the viewpoint of the **magnitude** of change, and the **time course response** to a given stimulus. This probably reflects the **elasticity of response** to various stimuli and human diversity itself, which is largely dictated by the underlying genetic matrix of the individual, together with the environment in which he/she is immersed (Norris and Smith, 2002).

Readiness

Readiness is another important factor in trainability. A child's level of growth, development and maturity will clearly determine the ability to perform certain tasks and meet demands in both training and competition. Tanner (1989) refers to readiness as the critical period in the development of a specific behaviour, when experience or training has an optimal effect on development. The same experience, introduced at an earlier or later time, has only limited effect, or retards later skill acquisition.

The factors affecting trainability may differ between body systems and fitness components. The common factors, listed by Bar-Or and Rowland (2004) are:

- age
- gender
- time elapsed from PHV
- body size and composition
- motor proficiency
- pre-training fitness level
- genotype
- interaction between genotype and the environment.

The following sections will focus on age, gender, body size (but not body composition), motor learning and PHV.

2. Windows of Trainability

Sensitive periods of trainability during the growth of young developing performers are often poorly, or not at all, recognised by coaches.

> When performers are biologically ready (that is, in the sensitive period for a specific domain), biological markers (see Figure 9) can help the coach identify the training components to be emphasised and those needing to be maintained or refined.

During sensitive periods, the external training load must be properly timed to achieve optimum adaptation with regards motor skills, speed, strength, stamina and suppleness.

Bar-Or and Rowland (2004, page 50) were the first scientists to refer to the concept of windows of trainability, which they called 'a window of opportunity for trainability'. Within sports coaching, this concept is often referred to as 'windows of optimal trainability'.

In their research, Viru (1995) and Viru et al (1998) highlighted the accelerated adaptation to physical training during periods of growth, development and maturation. Viru et al (1998) used 31 peer-reviewed studies and 11 reviews for meta-analyses to identify age periods of accelerated improvement in muscle strength, power, speed and endurance, in the age interval 6–18 years. In cross-sectional studies, the number of subjects varied from 83 to 21,175. In longitudinal studies, the variation was from 65–90. In terms of different physical skills, Viru et al concluded that between the ages of 6 and 18, different periods of accelerated improvement existed for different capabilities. These are given below.

- Speed and power:

  Males 7–9 years and 13–16 years

  Females 6–8 years and 11–13 years.

- Muscle strength and endurance:

There is only one common period for both sexes and it corresponds with the later stages of sexual maturation.

A number of references emphasise the importance of optimal trainability in physical skill training.

The International Gymnastics Federation's Age Group Development Programme identified five stages in the development of performers. These are: motor, physical, perceptual, cognitive and social/psychological, and include the:

- early childhood stage (up to 6 years of age)
- pre-pubertal stage (6–11 years of age)
- early pubertal stage (11–13 years of age)
- late pubertal stage (12–16 years of age)
- post-pubertal stage (15+ years).

The Programme's chapter on physical development is considered one of the most comprehensive reviews of trainability literature. Gymnastics is generally accepted to be an early specialisation sport (see Stafford, 2005, page 9 and Chapter 4 of this resource).

Malina and Bouchard (1991) provide an excellent overview of trainability in chapters relating to:

- motor development during infancy and childhood
- strength and motor performance during growth
- aerobic power and capability during growth
- anaerobic power and capability during growth.

Furthermore, Van Praagh (1998) offers profound insight into paediatric anaerobic performance, with various chapters identifying trainability and suggested periodised programmes for strength, power and speed development.

Although the sources listed above refer to the fact chronological and developmental age can be different, their data is based on chronological age. One interpretation of the data is, therefore, to use chronological age, but to combine this with key biological markers (see Figure 14) to identify developmental age (or maturation level) during puberty.

> The key biological markers are:
>
> - the onset of PHV
> - PHV itself
> - the onset of menarche.

It is possible to link the windows of optimal trainability to the five Ss of training and performance. Dick (2007) introduced the concept to overview training and performance needs.

> If coaches are aware of the key biological markers and can recognise the developmental stage of the young performer, they will be able to exploit the opportunities provided by the sensitive periods of accelerated adaptation to training.

The five Ss are:

- stamina (or endurance)
- strength
- speed
- skill
- suppleness (or flexibility).

There are several key issues for coaches to consider in relation to the five Ss.

1. Capabilities of stamina, strength, speed, skills and suppleness are always trainable. However, during the sensitive periods, accelerated adaptation will occur if the proper volume, intensity, frequency and choice of exercise are chosen or selected.

2. Improvements in different capabilities occur during adolescence without training. For example, VO_2 max (the measure of aerobic power) increases in boys by about 150% and by 80% in girls between the ages 8–16 (Armstrong and Welshman, 1995). Importantly, this increase occurs without regular physical activity, as it is related to growth.

3. Strength will increase by two thirds after PHV, again without regular physical activity, due to growth.

Given the information on windows of trainability, clearly implementing proper endurance and resistance training programmes during the sensitive periods of trainability will enhance adaptation and can contribute significantly to the foundation of aerobic and strength development.

Unfortunately, many coaches currently design long- and short-term training programmes (and models), as well as competition and recovery programmes, based on performers' chronological age.

> Research has shown chronological age is a poor basis for athlete development models, since the musculoskeletal, cognitive/mental and emotional development of performers between the ages of 8–16 can vary greatly within any given age category (Borms, 1986).

In addition, coaches who superimpose a scaled down adult version of a training and competition programme on a young developing performer are not acting in the best interests of the young performer in question.

Ideally, coaches should determine the maturity (ie developmental age) of their young performers and use this information as the foundation for performer-specific training, competition and recovery programmes. Unfortunately, as discussed in Chapter 2, there is no reliable procedure to identify biological maturity non-invasively. The dangers of using other procedures (eg X-rays) for assessing biological age have already been outlined in the previous chapter.

Chapter 2 also suggested some solutions to help coaches. One is to use the onset of PHV, and PHV itself, as reference points for the design of optimal, individual programmes, in relation to sensitive periods of trainability during the maturation process. Prior to the onset of PHV, boys and girls can train together and chronological age can be used to determine training, competition and recovery programmes.

> The onset of PHV is a reference point, providing valuable information for training the young developing performer. By using simple measurements (as described in Chapter 6), PHV can be monitored and training prioritised to exploit the sensitive periods of trainability. This approach can enhance the development of short- and long-term individually optimised training, competition and recovery programmes.

The average age for the onset of PHV in the UK is 8.5–10.5 years for females and 10.3–12.1 for males.

Windows of optimal trainability (and accelerated adaptation) for stamina (endurance), strength, speed, skill and suppleness (flexibility) training are shown in Figure 9. Coaches will note the different time frames for females and males.

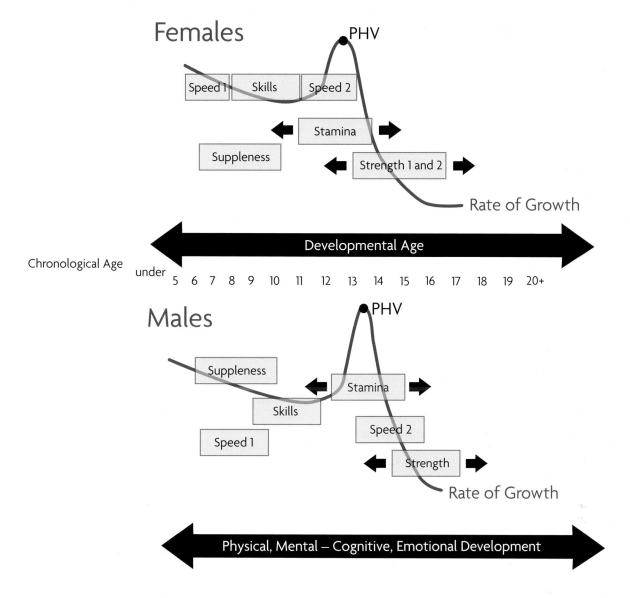

Figure 9: Windows of optimal trainability (adapted from Canadian Sport for Life, 2005)

The arrows in the above diagram indicate moving scales, which are dependent on growth patterns. Boxes without arrows are based on chronological age.

Please note, these windows are fully open during the sensitive periods of accelerated adaptation to training, and partially open outside such periods.

In the appendices at the end of this chapter, Appendix 2 (adapted from Vorontsov, 2002), Appendix 3 (Schramm, 1984) and Appendix 4 (Mero, 1998) all provide chronological age-based trainability models.

As previously noted, stamina, strength, speed, skill and suppleness are always trainable. However, during the sensitive periods of trainability, accelerated adaptation will occur if the proper volume, intensity, frequency and choice of exercise are selected.

Sections 3–7 outline the optimal trainability of each of the five Ss of training and performance.

3. Trainability of the Aerobic System (Stamina or Endurance)

The onset of PHV contributes to accelerated adaptation of the aerobic system, which is sometimes known as peak aerobic velocity (PAV).

Prior to puberty, children mainly improve the economy of their movement. This is reflected in a decrease in the oxygen cost of their physical activity, without an increase in VO_2 max. However, young people do increase their VO_2 max significantly after the onset of PHV, to a peak between 12–15 years of age for females, and 14–16 years of age for males. As mentioned previously, VO_2 peak for males increases by about 150% between the ages of 8–16. For girls, the increase is about 80% between the ages of 8–15.

After the onset of PHV, boys exhibit a spurt in VO_2 max that often occurs just after the greatest increase in height, corresponding with the advance of male hormone secretion. The steep rise in VO_2 max of boys continues until about 16 years of age. After this, a slower rise continues until about age 18.

In girls, VO_2 max reaches its peak around 14 years of age and a slow rise continues to age 16. This increase would also occur without training, as it is due to growth and maturation. Coaches can hypothesise about a possible increase in VO_2 max during this period, if a properly planned and structured training and recovery programme is implemented and monitored. In support of this idea, Kobayashi et al (1978) stated: 'Beginning approximately one year prior to PHV and thereafter, training effectively increased aerobic power above the normal increase attributable to age and growth.' Many leading coaches have experimented successfully with training programmes that emphasise the development of aerobic systems during this key period of development.

Beginning with the onset of PHV, sports that require a strong aerobic base – that is, most late specialisation sports (see Chapter 4) – should prioritise aerobic capacity with continuous exercise, such as long, slow distance, and fartlek or speed-play type training. When growth decelerates, aerobic power training (ie interval training) should be introduced. Sports requiring less of an aerobic base (eg artistic gymnastics, diving) should use ultra-short interval training to train the aerobic and anaerobic system in parallel. Aerobic capacity and power indirectly and directly contribute to enhanced quality of training time, help recovery between bouts of exercise/training sessions and help recovery in general. Aerobic capacity and power also play a significant role in environmental adaptations, such as altitude and jet lag, and assist with recovery from minor injuries. Thus, the extent of aerobic training should specifically be determined by individual sports (see Appendix 6 of this chapter) for energy system distribution.

Aerobic training programmes for females between 11 and 15 years of age, and males between 12 and 16, should be individualised, or performers grouped together for fitness preparation, after the onset of PHV.

Aerobic training should be based on maturation level, rather than chronological age. Young developing performers may be four to five years apart within an age group. After maturation, all systems are fully trainable. Diagnostics (testing or profiling) and sport-specific normative data will determine the extent of aerobic training needs.

In principle, early, average and late-maturing training groups (see Chapter 4) should be formed, so adaptation to fitness and skills training is based on maturation levels and not chronological age. Otherwise, under and overtraining can occur and only a small number of each chronological age group will be properly trained. In addition, the sensitive period of accelerated adaptation of the aerobic system could be compromised.

Grouping of all team members for parts of training is recommended. Removing young players from their age groups can have negative effects on emotional development and socialisation.

Performers' growing pains can be reduced, or better controlled, by using proper progressions of technical-tactical training and strength training involving weight-bearing activities. Aerobic training for this maturation level should consist of non-weight-bearing activity (eg swimming and cycling) if required.

Figure 10 (overleaf) shows the trainability of aerobic capacity and aerobic power for late specialisation sports.

> In the case of team sports, it is suggested teams should train together for technical and tactical training, but fitness preparation should be based on maturation levels and individual needs.

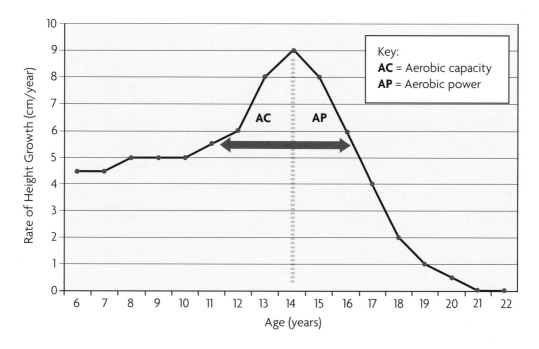

**Figure 10: The trainability of aerobic capacity and aerobic power for late specialisation sports
(Balyi and Way, 2005, unpublished PowerPoint slide)**

Aerobic capacity training emphasis should commence with the onset of PHV (no lactic acid accumulation or less than 4mml). After reaching PHV, when growth decelerates, aerobic power should be emphasised (lactic accumulation, lactate tolerance and lactate removal). Of course, the priority will be based on sport-specific needs.

As an example of aerobic trainability, the 1998 US Swimming Sport Science Summit (Lawrence, 1999) summarised aerobic trainability as follows:

- VO_2 max shows significant growth from 10–13 to 14 years of age and peaks between 17–21 years for males and 12–15 years for females.

- This time frame, when significant growth can occur (sensitive periods), should be maximised in training, to develop the swimmer's long-term potential.

- Pre-pubescent performers show significant improvements in long duration, low intensity events.

- Coaches should optimise aerobic training during this sensitive period.

- It is suggested pre-pubescent swimmers (ages 9–12/15) focus on swimming longer distances for reasons related to skill development and aerobic capacity development.

Vorontsov (2002), a former Soviet, now British, high-performance swimming coach and sport scientist, outlined his theory on sensitive periods of aerobic trainability in young performers:

- Training should be subdivided into stages, according to the timing and rhythm of individual growth and maturation.

- Pre-pubescent children are more predisposed to extensive aerobic training, since their heart size and blood volume increases in proportion to their body size. The peak increase in boys' heart size occurs at 13–14 years, with girls' at 11–12 years.

- Intensive training exercises should be applied with caution and their volume increased gradually.

- Purposeful training for the development of cardiorespiratory and vascular systems may be used effectively in pre-pubescent and early pubescent periods of individual development. This training aims to develop aerobic capacity and efficiency.

- The onset of the growth spurt and maturation is the most appropriate time for the development of aerobic power (VO_2 max).

- Training of maximal strength and anaerobic endurance will be most efficient in post-pubescent young performers.

The above recommendations suggest aerobic capacity be prioritised before puberty in non-weight-bearing aerobic sports. There is reasonable empirical evidence to show long-duration continuous activities, combined with skill training, can contribute significantly to the development of the aerobic base and sport-specific skills. For example, Rushall (1998) suggests the major content in swimming training should be distance work at a comfortable level (anaerobic threshold and below), with obvious concentration on skill, smoothness and mechanical efficiency.

Non-weight-bearing sports requiring a high aerobic base, such as swimming, rowing, canoeing and cycling, should prioritise aerobic capacity training with skill development, prior to the onset of PHV. Following the onset of PHV, the training priority for these types of sports should move from the development of aerobic capacity to aerobic power (see Figure 11a).

COACHING THE YOUNG DEVELOPING PERFORMER

Figures 11a and 11b schematically illustrate the differences between non-weight-bearing and weight-bearing sports in terms of aerobic capacity and power.

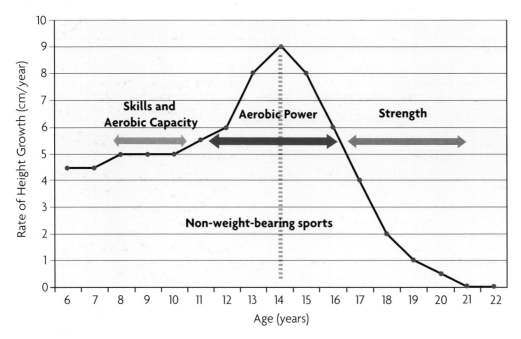

Figure 11a: Trainability in non-weight-bearing sports
(Balyi and Way, 2005, unpublished PowerPoint slide)

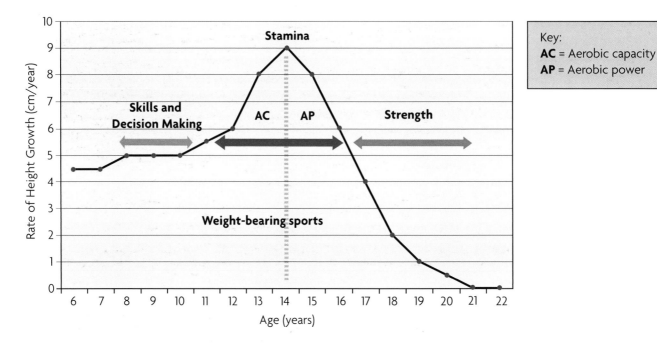

Figure 11b: Trainability in weight-bearing sports
(Balyi and Way, 2005, unpublished PowerPoint slide)

In weight-bearing sports requiring a significant energy contribution from the aerobic system, technical skills, tactical development and simple decision-making skills are important before the onset of the growth spurt. Development of the aerobic system is not a priority during this time. Sports such as football, basketball, volleyball and hockey would benefit from such an approach.

Performers in sports that do not require a high contribution of energy from aerobic sources, such as artistic gymnastics and diving, need to develop a sport-specific aerobic base. Aerobic capacity and power, however, will not be a high priority compared to other fitness factors.

The question for coaches should be: how much endurance training is enough? Answers given will depend on the sport. Appendix 6 identifies various sports and their predominant energy systems. The percentage contribution (during competition) of the ATP-PC, LA/O_2 and O_2 systems is identified. However, when training is considered in most sports, there will be a higher O_2 and LA/O_2 requirement, to assist recovery between bouts and intervals, between training sessions in a day, to recover from one day to the next, to help environmental acclimatisation (ie jet lag, altitude, heat and cold) and, finally, to accelerate performer recovery from minor injuries.

4. Trainability of Strength

Strength gains during pre-adolescence or before PHV are possible (Blimkie and Bar-Or, 1995). It appears children are as trainable as adolescents or young adults, though mainly with regards to relative strength (percentage improvements relative to own body weight) rather than absolute strength (Blimkie and Bar-Or, 1995). Strength training can be introduced at an early training age, using medicine balls and Swiss ball exercises for fun, to improve basic movement skills and general strength and power development.

Performers' body weight can also be used to increase strength. Shoulder, spine, hip, knee, ankle alignment and core stabilisation should be emphasised from early training ages, through fun activities. It is vital to stress the importance of core stabilisation at all training ages.

Strength gains before puberty will occur through motor learning, improvements in motor coordination, and through morphological and neurological adaptations. Exercise and increased muscle activation will also increase strength. Pre-puberty structural changes such as hypertrophy (increase in muscle mass) should not be expected.

Short-term strength training at this time does not seem to interfere with endurance activities (Blimkie and Sage, 1998). However, unlike adults, the maintenance of strength gains for pre-pubescent performers cannot be achieved with one session per microcycle (Blimkie and Sage, 1998). Frequency of training should be two or three times per week and duration should not exceed 30 minutes. The sensitive periods of accelerated adaptation to strength training will occur towards the end of, or immediately after, PHV (International Gymnastics Federation CD/DVD) and the onset of menarche for females, and 12–18 months after PHV for males (Anderson and Bernhardt, 1998, Lawrence, 1999 and Ross and Marfell-Jones, 1991).

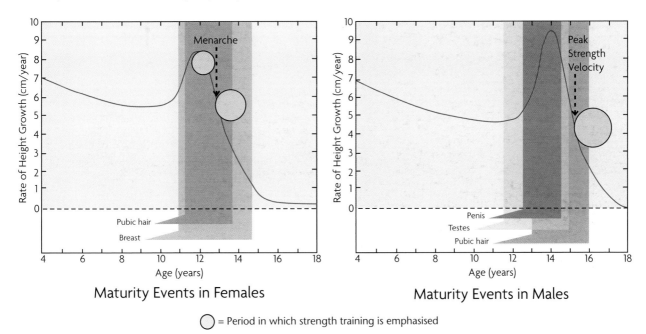

$\bigcirc$ = Period in which strength training is emphasised

Figure 12: The two windows for females immediately after PHV and at the onset of menarche, and the peak strength velocity 12–18 months after PHV for males (adapted from Ross and Marfell-Jones, 1991)

Females who increase body and muscle mass quickly should emphasise strength training by using weightlifting immediately after PHV. Those increasing body and muscle mass more slowly should emphasise strength training by using weightlifting with the onset of menarche, as full hormonal maturation will have been achieved. Males who increase body and muscle mass quickly should start with free weights 12 months after PHV. Those who increase muscle mass more slowly should begin 18 months after PHV.

Coaches should be aware that learning the correct weightlifting technique, prior to the window of optimal trainability for strength, will help performers avoid injuries and maximise the benefits of this sensitive period.

In sports where maximum strength plays an important role, Olympic lifting techniques (see Brewer, 2006) and free weights should be introduced. Olympic lifts are very technical. An early introduction to lifting techniques before PHV should prepare performers to avoid injuries and for optimal strength training, when required.

5. Trainability of Speed

Speed development incorporates linear, lateral, multi-directional, change of direction, agility and segmental speed. Two windows of accelerated adaptation to speed training are identified below:

- Females 6–8 years of age and 11–13 years of age

- Males 7–9 years of age and 13–16 years of age (Viru et al, 1998).

After undertaking a review of literature, Borms (1986) concluded that the rate of development of speed accelerates in two windows. The first window is around eight years of age for boys and girls. The second occurs around 12 years of age for girls and between 12–15 years for boys. These ages are very similar to Viru's meta-analysis on speed (Viru et al, 1998).

The first window for speed training for females and males is not concerned with training the energy system, but rather the central nervous system (CNS). This means the training of agility, quickness, change of direction and segmental speed develops through the CNS. The volume and duration of training is very low, but the CNS and, to some extent, the anaerobic alactic power system (see glossary) should be challenged. The duration of the exercise should be no more than five seconds. Full recovery should be achieved between sets and repetitions.

Anaerobic alactic power and anaerobic alactic capacity interval training should only start during the second window of accelerated adaptation to speed training. The duration of the exercise is recommended to be between 5–20 seconds and full recovery should be achieved between sets. The overall volume of training is low.

Interestingly, Cooper (1995) reported children were more often engaged in short bursts of intense activity exercise than in long-term activities. The average duration of this high-intensity activity was only six seconds, and the average interval between short-burst activities was about 20 seconds. This typical activity seems more of a natural pattern during growth, rather than extensively long exercise bouts.

> **Key Issues for the Trainability of Speed**
>
> - It is highly recommended speed should be trained on a regular and frequent basis. For example, at every training session after the warm-up.
> - Towards the end of the warm-up, or immediately after it, there is no central nervous system or metabolic fatigue. This is an optimal time to train speed.
> - Volume of training should be low and allow for full recovery between exercises and sets.
> - Acceleration should be over a short distance, with proper posture and elbow and knee drive emphasised.
> - Take-off speed and segmental speed should be trained regularly, outside of the window of optimal trainability for speed.
> - In addition to regular parts of the training session being set aside for speed development (such as the warm-up), proper blocks of training (ie block loading) should be allocated to speed training at all stages of development, at the proper time, in a periodised annual training plan.
> - Particular attention should be paid, by coaches, to the two speed windows of trainability.

6. Trainability of Movement and Sports Skill

FUNdamental movement skills and FUNdamental sports skills are most trainable between the ages of 5–12. Coordination and motor skills develop very well in physically active boys and girls during childhood, together with rapid development of the nervous system (Mero, 1998).

Tittel (1991) noted that individuals who were biologically younger (about 11 years of age) showed better coordination test results than those biologically aged 13–14 years. This shows coordinative maturity occurs before sexual maturation and is the main reason early specialisation sports (see Stafford, 2005, page 9) begin sport-specific training at five or six years of age. Performers need to acquire the necessary general and sport-specific skills before the onset of PHV. In late specialisation sports, intense training of specialised sports skills at an early age has more disadvantages than advantages. Early sport-specific training contributes to one-sided preparation, unbalanced fitness, which, together with early training of technical-tactical and sport-specific skills, means young performers do not develop the broader skill base necessary for a later stage of development.

Peak Motor Coordination Velocity

The accelerated adaptation to motor skills and coordination development from 8–11 years of age for females, and 9–11 years for males, is called peak motor coordination velocity (PMCV). Most experts agree with this sensitive period (Borms, 1986). Its importance is paramount to coaches and parents; both need to understand that FUNdamental movement and basic sport-specific skills should be acquired before ages 11 and 12 respectively. In more precise terms, it is most desirable to acquire movement and basic sport skills before the onset of the growth spurt. Specialising early in late specialisation sports tends to have negative consequences. There is a considerable body of evidence that shows early specialisation in late specialisation sports contributes to burnout and early retirement (Cote, 2007; Bompa, 2000 and Rushall, 1998).

Figure 13: FUNdamental sports skills (Canadian Sport for Life, 2005)

The photo set above illustrates some of the key FUNdamental movement skills children should acquire. Appendix 1 lists the wide variety of FUNdamental movement skills that underpin FUNdamental sports skills (Canadian Sport for Life, 2005).

Coaches should realise that, although skills are always trainable, skill trainability gradually declines after 11–12 years of age, or, more precisely, before the onset of the growth spurt. That is not to say it is impossible to improve skills after 12 years of age. Rather, the foundations for skill learning are laid before the onset of growth spurt, and if these foundations are not properly developed, it is harder to improve skills later in life, meaning development may be hindered. The skill windows for males and females are given below:

• Skills window for females: 8–11 years of age

• Skills window for males: 9–12 years of age.

It is recommended FUNdamental movement skills, such as the ABCs of athleticism (agility, balance, coordination and speed), and the ABCs of athletics (run, jump and throw), be introduced in a child-friendly environment through fun and games activities in the early stages of the skills window (usually from six years of age). As children become more confident and competent with these underpinning movement skills, they can progress to a wide variety of FUNdamental sports skills (ie the basic sports skills that are often introduced, using adapted equipment and a mini-game approach). For late specialisation sports, it is important children and young people sample a wide variety of FUNdamental sports skills. This has been shown to be more conducive to long-term development, once performers are specialising in a particular sport (usually between 13–15 years of age).

7. Trainability of Suppleness (Flexibility)

Suppleness (or flexibility) is a key training and performance capability. Optimal individual and sport-specific flexibility should be established at an early training age. However, there is limited information available on how best to develop flexibility and of how training of flexibility affects children. In principle, training for increased joint mobility should start before the onset of PHV (Armstrong et al, 1997 and Mero, 1998). According to Mero, the ages of nine and 12 years (before puberty) are a sensitive phase for flexibility training. This is the phase when maximum levels of flexibility can be achieved.

During, and immediately after, PHV, monitoring of flexibility is important, as rapidly growing bones stretch muscles, tendons and ligaments. Optimal sport and individual specific flexibility ranges should be maintained during the growth spurt. Flexibility should form part of the regular musculoskeletal screening of the pubertal growth spurt.

Appendix 5 illustrates the vulnerability of certain parts of the body to injury during the growth spurt. This is vital information for coaches needing to take account of how a particular training programme may overstress a vulnerable part of the body during this spurt.

Prior to the onset of PHV, it is recommended dynamic mobility and static stretching be emphasised. It is also advisable not to stretch during rest days in a training cycle.

If flexibility requires improvement, it is recommended flexibility training should be undertaken five to six times per week. If current flexibility levels are to be maintained, two to three sessions of flexibility training each week, or training every other day, is advisable.

Static stretching should not form part of the warm-up, as it does not prevent injury. Fitness, on the other hand, does (Shrier, 1999). In principle, static stretching and proprioceptive neuromuscular facilitation (PNF) should be performed two hours prior to, or two hours after, training and/or competition.

8. Summary of Trainability

The windows of trainability outlined in this chapter indicate the priorities for different fitness capabilities (ie the five Ss) within the various stages of long-term athlete development. Challenges for the coach working with young developing performers are to:

- measure and monitor the key reference points through the onset of PHV to adulthood, for individual performers

- take account of the biological markers to help make decisions (see Figure 14)

- design an appropriate programme for each performer, which will take advantage of the windows of trainability and be based on sport-specific training needs.

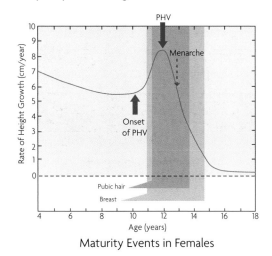
Maturity Events in Females

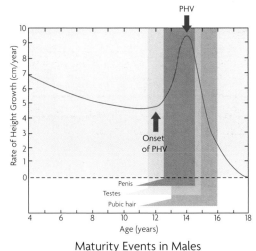
Maturity Events in Males

Figure 14: The biological markers (adapted from Canadian Sport for Life, 2005)

Key Concepts and Summary

Windows of Optimal Trainability

- Stamina, strength, speed, skill and suppleness are always trainable. However, the rate of improvement is influenced by the sensitive periods of trainability and/or maturation levels.

- Three windows of trainability are based on chronological age. These are: skill, speed and suppleness (because all research is based on chronological age).

- Two windows are based on the individual's tempo of growth and biological maturity. These are: stamina and strength.

- Biological markers requiring consideration are the onset of PHV, PHV itself, and the onset of menarche.

9. Conclusion

This chapter has attempted to identify the complex maturational process in young developing performers, with regards adaptation and trainability. The intention has been to give coaches information on the development of the five Ss of training and performance at different ages. In addition, biological markers have been identified to help coaches decide when a change of emphasis in a developmental training plan for a young developing performer is necessary.

The key biological and growth markers have been identified as:

- the onset of PHV

- PHV

- the onset of menarche.

Figure 14 shows the time frames when these biological markers are important. Monitoring the individual performer's growth and development patterns with these markers gives the coach relevant information on when to adapt the training programme, to ensure windows of trainability are fully utilised.

Viru (1995) noted a crucial factor for coaches designing programmes for young performers going through the maturation process. He stated: 'If there is conflict between long-term development and the demands of competition, the first must take priority (page 205).' This is a vital message for coaches. Competition and performance demands should not interfere with the optimisation of training processes (see Chapter 5 case studies). If there is interference, performers will miss key stages in the development of physical capabilities and skills. They are, therefore, unlikely to realise their full potential. It can be argued this principle of de-emphasising the importance of competition links well with a way to minimise the relative age effect outlined in Chapter 4. That is to say, for a late maturer, extra emphasis on fitness and skill development will enable the performer to catch up with the early maturer. Additionally, there will be a reduction in the negative effects of experiencing disappointing performance results in the short term.

The key message for coaches from this chapter is the importance of prioritising, integrating and sequencing training and competition activities for young performers, in relation to individual growth, development and maturation. The training gains offered by using the windows of trainability for the five Ss of training and performance provide coaches with a method of working that ultimately helps young developing performers reach their full potential. It makes sense, therefore, that periodised training and competition, and recovery, programmes for young developing performers should be adapted for the individual, as soon as the coach is able to monitor growth and development patterns.

Appendix 1

Appendix 1 lists the wide variety of fundamental movements and skills that underpin physical literacy. They include four different environments: earth, water, air and ice.

Travelling Skills	Object Control Skills	Balance Movements
• Boosting	**Sending:**	• Balancing/centring
• Climbing	• Kicking	• Body Rolling
• Eggbeater	• Punting	• Dodging
• Galloping	• Rolling (ball)	• Eggbeater
• Gliding	• Strike (ball, puck, ring)	• Floating
• Hopping	• Throwing	• Landing
• Ice Picking	**Receiving:**	• Ready position
• Jumping	• Catching	• Sinking/Falling
• Leaping	• Stopping	• Spinning
• Poling	• Trapping	• Stopping
• Running	**Travelling with:**	• Stretching/Curling
• Sculling	• Dribbling (feet)	• Swinging
• Skating	• Dribbling (hands)	• Twisting/Turning
• Skipping	• Dribbling (stick)	
• Sliding	**Receiving and Sending:**	
• Swimming	• Striking (bat)	
• Swinging	• Striking (stick)	
• Wheeling	• Volleying	

(Adapted from Canadian Sport for Life, 2005)

Appendix 2

Sensitive periods for development of motor abilities in young swimmers (adapted from Vorontsov, 2002)
(Vorontsov, Solomatin and Sidorov, 1986, 1988)

Boys	8	9	10	11	12	13	14	15	16	17	18
Coordination/Agility	▒	▒	▒	▒	█	█	▒				
Flexibility/Mobility	▒	▒	▒	█	█	█	▒				
Aerobic Capacity		▒	▒	█	█	█	█	▒	▒	▒	
Aerobic Power					▒	█	█	█	█	▒	
Anaerobic Abilities				▒	▒	▒	█	█	█	█	▒
Speed/Strength				▒	▒	▒	█	█	█	█	█
Maximal Strength						▒	█	█	█	█	█
General Strength Endurance		▒	▒	▒	█	█	█	█	█	▒	▒
Special Strength Endurance					▒	█	█	█	█	█	▒
Pulling Force				▒	█	█	█	█	█	█	▒

Girls	8	9	10	11	12	13	14	15	16	17	18
Coordination/Agility	▒	▒	█	█	█	▒					
Flexibility/Mobility	▒	█	█	█	█	▒					
Aerobic Capacity	▒	█	█	█	█	█	▒	▒			
Aerobic Power			▒	█	█	█	█	▒			
Anaerobic Abilities				▒	█	█	█	█	▒		
Speed/Strength				▒	▒	█	█	█	█		
Maximal Strength				▒	█	█	█	█	█		
General Strength Endurance	▒	▒	█	█	█	█	█	▒			
Special Strength Endurance				▒	█	█	█	█	▒	▒	▒
Pulling Force			▒	█	█	█	█	▒	▒	▒	

Appendix 3

Sensitive periods for development of motor abilities in young swimmers, according to Schramm et al, 1984
(adapted from Vorontsov, 2002)

Boys	8	9	10	11	12	13	14	15	16	17	18
Coordination/Agility	■	■	■	■	■	▨					
Rapidness/Motor Reaction	■	■	■	■	■	■					
Speed of Locomotions			■	■	■	■	■	■	▨		
Extensive Aerobic Endurance	■	■	■	■	■	■	■	▨	▨	▨	▨
Intensive Aerobic Endurance				▨	■	■	■	■	▨	▨	
General Strength Endurance	■	■	■	■	■						
Rapid Strength (small resistance)				■	■						
Maximal Strength						▨	■	■	■	■	■
Special Strength Endurance					■	■	■	■	■	■	■

Girls	8	9	10	11	12	13	14	15	16	17	18
Coordination/Agility	■	■	■	■	▨						
Rapidness/Motor Reaction	■	■	■	■	■						
Speed of Locomotions			■	■	■	■	▨				
Extensive Aerobic Endurance	■	■	■	■	■	▨	▨	■			
Intensive Aerobic Endurance			■	■	■	■	▨	▨	▨		
General Strength Endurance	■	■	■	■	■						
Rapid Strength (small resistance)			■	■	■						
Maximal Strength					▨	■	■	■	■	■	■
Special Strength Endurance				■	■	■	■	■	■	■	■

Appendix 4

Mero's table (Van Praagh, 1998, adapted from Mero et al 1990. Reprinted with permission from Mero, 1998.)
The important training areas (sensitive phases) at different ages

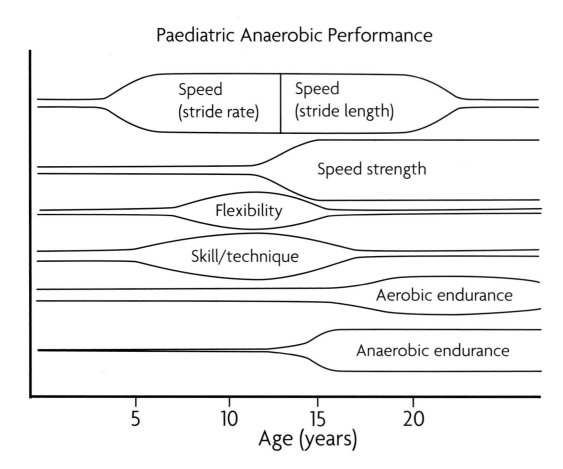

Paediatric Anaerobic Performance

Appendix 5

Specific periods of vulnerabilty for the developing bones. For boys, this period is approximately two years later (Klein, 2002)

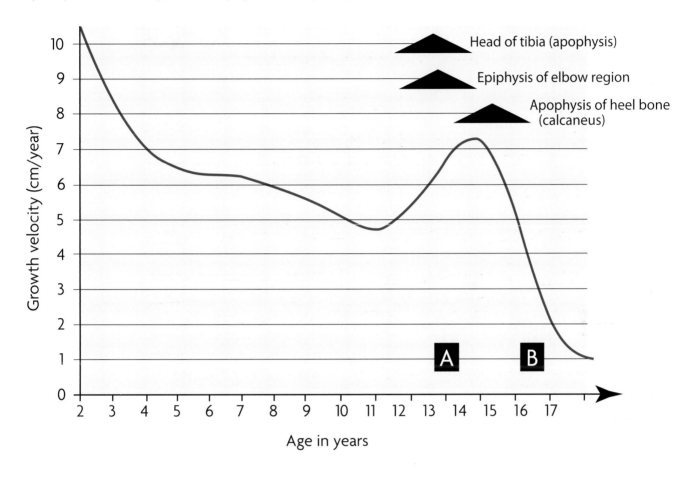

Key:
A = Time period of vulnerability
B = Time period of diminshing vulnerability

LIVERPOOL JOHN MOORES UNIVERSITY
LEARNING SERVICES

Appendix 6

Various sports and their predominant energy systems

Sports or Sport Activity		% Emphasis According to Energy Systems		
		ATP-PC and LA	LA-O_2	O_2
1. Baseball		80	20	-
2. Basketball		85	15	-
3. Fencing		90	10	-
4. Field hockey		60	20	20
5. Football		90	10	-
6. Golf		95	5	-
7. Gymnastics		90	10	-
8. Ice hockey	a. Forwards, defence	80	20	-
	b. Goalie	95	5	-
9. Lacrosse	a. Goalie, defence, attack men	80	20	-
	b. Midfielders, man-down	60	20	20
10. Rowing		20	30	50
11. Skiing	a. Slalom, jumping, downhill	80	20	-
	b. Cross-country	-	5	95
	c. Pleasure skiing	34	33	33
12. Soccer	a. Goalie, wings, strikers	80	20	-
	b. Halfbacks, or link men	60	20	20
13. Swimming and diving	a. 50 yds, diving	98	2	-
	b. 100 yds	80	15	5
	c. 200 yds	30	65	5
	d. 400, 500 yds	20	40	40
	e. 1500, 1650 yds	10	20	70
14. Tennis		70	20	10
15. Track and field	a. 100, 220 yds	98	2	-
	b. Field events	90	10	-
	c. 440 yds	80	15	5
	d. 880 yds	30	65	5
	e. 1 mile	20	55	25
	f. 2 miles	20	40	40
	g. 3 miles	10	20	70
	h. 6 miles (cross-country)	5	15	80
	i. Marathon	-	5	95
16. Volleyball		90	10	-
17. Wrestling		90	10	-

(Adapted from Fox and Matthews, 1974)

References

Anderson, G. and Bernhardt, T. (1998) 'Coaching children: growth and maturation considerations,' *BC Coaches Perspective*. Fall 1998: 14–15.

Armstrong, N. and Welshman, J. (1997) 'Children in sport and exercise', *British Journal of Physical Education*, 28 (2): 4–6.

Bar-Or, O. and Rowland, T. (2004) *Paediatric Exercise Medicine*. Champaign, Illinois: Human Kinetics. ISBN: 978-0-880115-97-1.

Blimkie, C.J.R. and Bar-Or, O. (1995) 'Trainability of muscle strength, power and endurance during childhood', in Bar-Or, O. (ed) (1995) *The Child and Adolescent Athlete*. Oxford: Blackwell Science Ltd: ISBN: 978-0-865429-04-8.

Blimkie, C. and Sage, D. (1998) 'Strength development and trainability during childhood', in Van Praagh, E. (1998) *Pediatric Anaerobic Performance*. Champaign, Illinois: Human Kinetics. ISBN: 978-0-873229-81-4.

Bompa T. (1985) 'Talent identification', *Sports Science Periodical on Research and Technology in Sport*, GN-1, February: 1–11.

Bompa, T. (2000) *Total Training for Young Champions*. Champaign, Illinois: Human Kinetics. ISBN: 978-0736002-12-7.

Borms, J. (1986) 'The Child and exercise: an overview,' *Journal of Sport Sciences*, 4: 3–20.

Bouchard, C., Malina, R.M. and Perusse, L. (1997) *Genetics of Fitness and Physical Performance*. Champaign, Illinois: Human Kinetics. ISBN: 978-0-873229-51-7.

Brewer, C. (2006) 'Strength and Conditioning' posters. Leeds: Coachwise Business Solutions/The National Coaching Foundation.

Canadian Sport for Life (2005) 'Long-term Athlete Development resource paper v2', Canadian Sport for Life. ISBN: 0-9738274-0-8.

Canadian Sport for Life (2009) 'Trainability', www.canadiansportforlife.ca/default.aspx?PageID=1044&LangID=en

Cooper, D.M. (1995) 'New horizons in pediatric exercise science research', in Blimkie, J. and Bar-Or, O. (1995) *New Horizons in Pediatric Exercise Science*. Leeds: Human Kinetics Europe Ltd. ISBN: 978-0-873225-28-1.

Cote, J. (2007) 'Pathways for Beginner to Elite to Ensure Optimum and Lifelong Involvement in Sport,' Presentation at sports coach UK melting pot. Leeds. January 2007.

Dick, F. (2007) *Sports Training Principles*. London: A & C Black Publishers Ltd. ISBN: 978-0-713682-78-6.

Fox, E.L., Bowers, R.W. and Foss, M.L. (1988) *The Physiological Basis of Physical Educational and Athletics*. Philadelphia: Saunders.

Fox, E.L. and Matthews, D. (1974) 'Interval training: Conditioning for sports and general fitness', in Fox, E.L., Bowers, R.W. and Foss, M.L (1988) *The Physiological Basis of Physical Educational and Athletics*. Philadelphia: Saunders.

Gallahue, D.L. and Ozmun, J.C. (2006) *Understanding Motor Development: Infants, Children, Adolescents, Adults*. Maidenhead: McGraw-Hill. ISBN: 978-0-071244-44-2.

Harris, J.A., Jackson, C.M., Paterson, D.G. and Scammon, R.E. (eds) (1930) 'Measurement of Body in Childhood' in *The Measurement of Man*. Minneapolis: University of Minnesota.

International Gymnastics Federation (no date) Age Group Development Programme. (CD/DVD)

Klein, N.W. (2002) Strength and conditioning for youth: paper presented at the Hong Kong Sports Institute annual coaching seminar. (PowerPoint presentation)

Kobayashi, K., Kitamura, K., Miura, M., Sodeyama, H., Murase, Y., Miyahita, M. and Matsui, H. (1978) 'Aerobic power as related to body growth and training in Japanese boys: a longitudinal study', *Journal of Applied Physiology*, Vol 44, 5: 666–672.

Lawrence, M. (1999) US Swimming Sport Science Summit for Young Swimmers: Learning about Athlete Development. (PowerPoint presentation)

MacDougall, J.D., Wenger, H.A. and Green, H.J. (eds) (1990) *Physiological testing of the high performance athlete* (second edition). Champaign, Illinois: Human Kinetics. ISBN: 978-0-873223-00-3.

Malina, R.M. and Bouchard, C. (1991) *Growth, Maturation and Physical Activity*. Champaign, Illinois: Human Kinetics. ISBN: 0-873223-21-7.

Mero, A. (1998) 'Power and speed training during childhood', in Van Praagh, E. (ed) (1998) *Paediatric Anaerobic Performance*, pp.252. Champaign, Illinois: Human Kinetics. ISBN: 978-0-873229-81-4.

Mero, A., Vuorimaa, T. and Hakkinen, K. (eds) (1990) *Training in Children and Adolescents*. Jyvaskyla, Finland: Gummerus Kirjapaino Oy

Morris, J.G. and Nevill, M.E. (2007) Sportnation. Loughborough University.

Nadori, L. (1985) *Az Edzes Elmelete Es Modszertana*. Budapest: Sport.

Norris, S.R. and Smith, D.J. (2002) 'Planning, periodisation and sequencing of training and competition: the rationale for a competently planned, optimally executed training and competition programme, supported by a multidisciplinary team', in Kellmann, M. (ed) *Enhancing Recovery: Preventing Underperformance in Athletes*. Champaign, Illinois. Human Kinetics. ISBN: 978-0-736034-00-5.

Ross, W.D. and Marfell-Jones, M.J. (1991) 'Kinanthropometry,' in MacDougall, J.D, Wenger, H.A. and Green, H.J. (eds) (1991) *Physiological testing of the high performance athlete* (second edition). Champaign, Illinois: Human Kinetics. ISBN: 978-0-873223-00-3.

Rushall, B. (1998) 'The Growth of Physical Characteristics in Male and Female Children', in *Sports Coach*, Vol.20, Summer: 25–27.

Scammon, R.E. (ed) (1930) 'Measurement of Body in Childhood' in *The Measurement of Man*. Minneapolis: University of Minnesota.

Schramm (1984) in Vorontsov, M.A. (2002) 'Development of Endurance in Young Swimmers', paper presented at the Vancouver BC Swimming Coaches Seminar. (PowerPoint presentation)

Shrier (1999) 'Stretching before exercise does not reduce the risk of local muscle injury', *Clinical Journal of Sport Medicine*, 9: 221–227.

Stafford, I. (2005) *Coaching for Long-term Athlete Development: to improve participation and performance in sport.* Leeds: Coachwise Business Solutions/The National Coaching Foundation. ISBN: 978-1-902523-70-5.

Tanner, J.M. (1989) *Foetus into Man: Physical Growth from Conception to Maturity.* Hertfordshire: Castlemead Publications. ISBN: 978-0-948555-24-4.

Tihanyi, J. (1990) *Long-term Planning for Young Performers: An Overview of the Influences of Growth, Maturation and Development.* Sudbury: Laurentian University.

Tittel, K. (1991) 'Coordination and balance', in Dirix, A., Knuttgen, H.G. and Tittel, K. *The Olympic Book of Sport Medicine.* Oxford: Blackwell Scientific. ISBN: 978-0-632030-84-2.

Ulster Council (2006) *Fun to Fame: Train to Train.* Armagh: Ulster Council GAA.

Van Praagh, E (ed) (1998) *Paediatric Anaerobic Performance.* Champaign, Illinois: Human Kinetics. ISBN: 978-0-873229-81-4.

Viru, A. (1995) *Adaptation in Sports Training.* CRC Press: Boca Raton. ISBN: 978-0-849301-71-1.

Viru, A. (1993) 'Mobilisation of the possibilities of the athlete's organism: a problem, *'The Journal of Sport Medicine and Physical Fitness'.* Vol.33 (4).

Viru, A., Loko, J., Volver, A., Laaneots, L., Karlesom, K. and Viru, M. (1998) 'Age periods of accelerated improvements of muscle strength, power, speed and endurance in age interval 6–18 years', in *Biology of Sport*, 15 (4): 211–227.

Viru, A. and Viru, M. (1993) 'The specific nature of training on muscle: a review,' *Sports Medicine, Training and Rehabilitation* (4): 79–98.

Vorontsov, M.A. (2002) 'Development of Endurance in Young Swimmers', paper presented at the Vancouver BC Swimming Coaches Seminar. (PowerPoint presentation)

Further Reading

Balyi, I. (no date) 'Sport system building and long-term athlete development in Canada: the situation and solutions', in *Coaches Report: The Official Publication of the Canadian Professional Coaches Association*, Summer 2001, Volume 8, No.1: 25–28.

Barnsley R.H., Thompson, A.H., Barnsley, P.E. (1985) 'Hockey success and birthdate: the relative age effect', *Journal of the Canadian Association for Health, Physical Education and Recreation*, Nov–Dec: 23–28.

Barnsley R.H. and Thompson, A.H. (1988) 'Birthdate and success in minor hockey: the key to the NHL', *Canadian Journal of Behavioural Science* 20:167–176.

Barnsley R.H., Thompson, A.H. and Legault, P. (1992) 'Family planning: football style and the relative age effect in football', *International Review for the Sociology of Sport*, 27 (1): 77–88.

Bar-Or, O. (1983) Paediatric sport medicine for the practitioner: from physiologic principles to clinical applications. New York: Springer Verlag.

Bar-Or, O. (ed) (1995) *The Child and the Adolescent Athlete.* Oxford: Blackwell Science Ltd. ISBN: 978-0-865429-04-8.

Bar-Or, O. (2000) 'Nutritional considerations for the child athlete', *Canadian Journal of Applied Physiology.* 26 (Suppl.): 186–191.

Baxter-Jones, A.D. (1995) 'Growth and development of young performers', *Sport Medicine*, 20: 59–64.

Beunen and Malina (no date) 'Growth and biological maturation: relevance to athletic performance', in Bar-Or, O. (ed) (1995) *The Child and Adolescent Athlete.* Oxford: Blackwell Science Ltd: ISBN: 978-0-865429-04-8.

Blimkie, C.J.R. and Marion, A. (1994) 'Resistance training during pre-adolescence: issues, controversies and recommendations', *Coaches Report*, Vol.1. No.4: 10–14.

Malina, R.M. and Bouchard, C. (1993) *Growth, Maturation and Physical Activity.* Champaign, Illinois: Human Kinetics. ISBN: 978-0-873223-21-8.

MacDougall, J.D., Wenger, H.A. and Green, H.J. (eds) (1991) *Physiological Testing of the High Performance Athlete* (second edition). Champaign, Illinois: Human Kinetics. ISBN: 978-0-873223-00-3.

Morris, J.G and Nevill, M.E. (2007) A sporting chance – enhancing opportunities for high-level sporting performance: influence of relative age. Loughborough University.

Tanner, J.M. (1973) 'Growing Up', *Scientific American*, 9.

Thumm, H-P. (1987) 'The importance of the basic training for the development of performance', *New Studies in Athletics*, Volume 1: 47–64.

Touretski, G. (1993) 'Physiological development of the young swimmer: a rationale for the long-term preparation of the young swimmer' (unpublished paper), *Australian Institute of Sport*.

Viru, A., Loko, J., Harro, M., Volver, A., Laaneots, L., Viru, M. (1999) 'Critical periods in the development of performance capacity during childhood and adolescence,' *Physical Education and Sport Pedagogy*, 4 (1): 75–119.

Wilmore, J.H. and Costill, D.L. (2005) *Physiology of Sport and Exercise.* Champaign, Illinois: Human Kinetics. ISBN: 978-0-736062-26-8.

Chapter 4: Key Coaching Issues Concerning Growth and Maturation of the Young Developing Performer

Istvan Balyi and Graham Ross

Introduction

This chapter brings together specific issues that impact on the coach's ability to understand and monitor growth and maturation of young developing performers. The information contained within will help coaches plan appropriate training, competition and recovery programmes.

Chapter 3 discussed the trainability of the five Ss of training and performance, namely stamina, strength, speed, skill and suppleness. This chapter will examine, in more detail, the practical issues coaches need to understand and consider when planning for, and working with, young developmental performers. These are:

1. early and late specialisation

2. early and late maturation

3. relative age effect

4. phases of growth and measurement.

1. Early and Late Specialisation

Reference has already been made to early and late specialisation sports (Stafford, 2005 and Canadian Sport for Life, 2005). Sports can generally be placed into these two categories based on training requirements for the development of elite performers. Such training requirements impact on the planning and implementation of programmes that can, and should, be developed. In general, the differences become apparent in the ages at which sport-specific skills are taught.

> Early specialisation incorporates individual sports such as gymnastics, rhythmic gymnastics, diving, figure skating and table tennis. These sports have high levels of specific skill, which must be learnt early for later success. Other sports such as track and field, tennis and rowing are late specialisation. For these sports, research deems a broader and more general base of training necessary for later success. Development of general physical and skill base is important before sport-specific skills are learnt.

Research also supports the idea that early specialisation in a late specialisation sport can lead to early burnout, and even drop out (Bompa, 2000). Bompa (1985) believes 'athletes who specialised at an early age had achieved their best results at junior age level. These performances were never duplicated when they became seniors'.

> When planning programmes, it is paramount the coach identifies whether a sport is early or late specialisation, to ensure the development of potential. (Note: Many sports provide guidance on athlete/player development models and programmes.)

2. Early and Late Maturation

Chapter 3 discussed the windows of trainability and the sensitive periods for young performers in the five Ss of training and performance (Figure 9). Gender differences between the sensitive periods were also considered in pages 10–12.

This section will discuss the different rates of growth and maturation in individual performers of the same age, illustrating these differences with a case study. This will show the pathways necessary for young performers, all of whom need to use the windows of trainability to ensure potential is reached. It is worth considering such performers will mature at different ages.

Figure 15 below shows the differences in rates of growth between early, average and late maturers at the age of 12 for girls and 14 for boys. It illustrates the real differences that exist in maturation rates. These rates can vary by as much as four years (Borms, 1986).

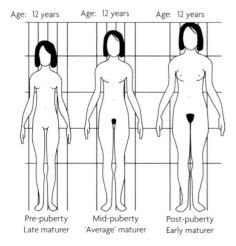
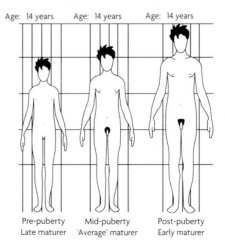

| Age: 12 years | Age: 12 years | Age: 12 years | | Age: 14 years | Age: 14 years | Age: 14 years |

| Pre-puberty
Late maturer | Mid-puberty
'Average' maturer | Post-puberty
Early maturer | | Pre-puberty
Late maturer | Mid-puberty
'Average' maturer | Post-puberty
Early maturer |

Figure 15: Late, average and early maturers (adapted from Canadian Sport for Life, 2005)

Figure 16 builds on the notion of the consequences of early and late maturation for training priorities in late specialisation sports, for two performers of the same chronological age (14). It shows the timing of aerobic capacity, aerobic power and strength training priorities in relation to the onset of PHV and PHV itself.

By comparing the two graphs, it can be seen how training priorities should be different for two performers of the same chronological age, but for one who is an early developer and the other a late. Readiness is the key issue in both cases. This concept was discussed in Chapter 3.

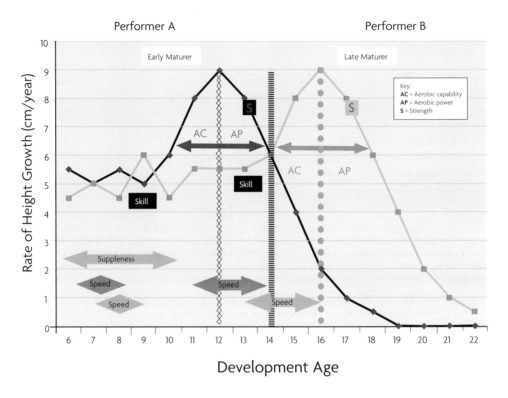

Figure 16: Readiness and training priorities, aerobic capability, aerobic power and strength (Balyi and Way, 2005)

The characteristics of the two performers are important, since they affect all the capabilities (aerobic capacity, aerobic power and strength) listed above.

- Both are chronologically aged 14 years.

- Performer A is an early maturer who started the growth spurt at 10 years of age and reached PHV at 12 years of age.

- Performer B is a late maturer who started the growth spurt at 14 years of age and reached PHV at 16 years of age.

If training programmes for these two performers are based on chronological age, neither will benefit unless programmes are properly individualised. Performer A (the early maturer) will be undertrained and Performer B (the late maturer) overtrained. The following case study explains in more depth the key features of overtraining and undertraining that would occur with Performer A and Performer B.

Aerobic Capacity, Aerobic Power and Strength Training

- In the case of Performer A, undertraining of the aerobic and strength system will occur. This is because, for the early maturer, the sensitive periods for both occur in terms of developmental age a few years **in advance** of the average maturer. Therefore, neither sensitive period will be fully exploited and optimal training will not be achieved. The extent of the aerobic system and strength training will be determined by sport-specific needs (ie whether the sport is aerobic or non-aerobic in nature, see Chapter 3, Appendix 5), so the significance of this issue will vary between sports.

- In the case of Performer B, fatigue will occur with less than optimal training of both the aerobic systems and strength. This is because, for the late maturer, the sensitive periods for aerobic capacity, aerobic power and strength training occur, in terms of developmental age, a few years **after** the average maturer. So, if Performer B follows a training programme based on chronological age, this will lead to the training load being poorly synchronised with the sensitive periods. In turn, this will have an impact on other training factors and, as a result, optimal adaptation will be inhibited.

- In overall terms, it is clear that to base a training programme for either Performer A or B on what the stimuli should be for the average maturer, based on chronological age, will not have an optimal effect. This is because:

  – Performer A should be undertaking a training programme that emphasises aerobic capacity when the priority should be aerobic power

- Performer B should be undertaking a training programme that emphasises aerobic power when the priority should be aerobic capacity

- Performer A should be undertaking a training programme that emphasises maximum strength training around 13–14 years of age, but which will only do so between 14–15 years of age (assuming 14 as the chronological age)

- Performer B should start maximum strength training around 17–18 years of age, but will actually do so around 15–16 years of age. Again, the performer will experience fatigue with less than optimal training effects, which will impact on other training factors.

Speed Training

Although speed should be trained all year round, its planning and implementation will be a challenge for both performers, since all scientific data is based on chronological age.

- Performer A will be developmentally more ready for speed training after PHV (at this age, speed training is for the energy system through interval training). The duration of the intervals is 15–20 seconds.

- Performer B should developmentally still be training speed for less than five seconds, prior to PHV, to improve agility, quickness, change of direction, acceleration and segmental speed, with limited energy system training.

- The average 14-year-old performer will exploit the window of accelerated adaptation to speed training the best. Neither Performer A or B is average, so less than optimal adaptation will occur.

Suppleness

This should be carefully monitored during PHV. The maintenance of the established range of motion is essential. Temporary loss of balance and coordination, due to sudden and rapid growth during PHV, should be explained to performers and parents. They should also understand that because of leg growth, longer levers will contribute to speed loss, acceleration and segmental speed. The following factors also need to be considered.

- For Performer A, suppleness, together with skill development, can be emphasised before the onset of PHV (ie up to 10 years of age developmentally). Thereafter, careful monitoring and evaluation during PHV can occur, to determine any loss of coordination and suppleness.

- For Performer B, there is an opportunity for suppleness and a focus on further skill development before the onset of PHV (ie up to 13 years of age developmentally). This gives Performer B further time to hone FUNdamental movement skills, sport-specific technical skills, decision-making skills and maintain levels of flexibility.

Clearly, all the training activities discussed in this case study should be properly sequenced and integrated within the framework of an annual individualised periodised plan.

For example, the emphasis on aerobic capability for Performers A and B, in relation to the other four Ss, will be different during the general preparatory, specific preparatory, pre-competitive and competitive phases of the periodised plan. Furthermore, sport-specific needs and demands will determine the percentage contribution of the five Ss within the annual plan. The technique of sequencing, integrating and quantifying training, competition and recovery programmes is clearly important, bearing in mind windows of optimum trainability and the sensitive periods.

3. Relative Age Effect

Coaches will be familiar with junior sport in terms of its competitive structures. From a practical standpoint, in order to organise training, competition and recovery programmes, most sports have age group competition at least to age 18, and sometimes to age 21. This means that to compete in a particular age group, young performers must be of a specific chronological age. For example, 16 and under. In practice, performers are of the same chronological age for a 12-month period – that is, the 14 and under age group is only open to performers between 13 and 14 years of age. In the UK, the 12-month period will usually coincide with either the school year (beginning on 1 September), or the calendar year (beginning on 1 January).

From the information already discussed on growth and maturation, coaches will then identify the following issues:

- Young performers under 18 or even 21 do not mature according to chronological age (see 'Early and Late Maturation' on page 39). Consequently, in any chronological age group, young performers can be up to four years apart developmentally. Yet all performers (whether early, average or late maturers) will be competing against, and training with, each other when grouping by age is the fundamental method of organisation.

- Whether a performer is an early or late maturer is compounded further by relative age. The consequences are severe for young performers in most sports. Many sports show successful performers are those born in the first half of the competitive year and that this success can be seen at senior level as well. One reason for this is that in each age group, the factor of early or late maturity can be further compounded by an additional 12-month period of chronological difference between performers. For example, two performers can both be in the competitive group for 14 and under, but one can become 14 on 1 January and the other on 31 December, adding 12 months to the real difference between them. In sports where age grouping is based on the school year, the same exists. One performer can be 14 years of age on 1 September and another reach the same age on 31 August. However, for 12 months they will be competing in the same age group. A recent study by Morris and Nevill (2007) drew attention both to the issue of relative age and to the outcomes for many sports. Many countries and sports can offer examples of relative age effect and its impact on selection and participation.

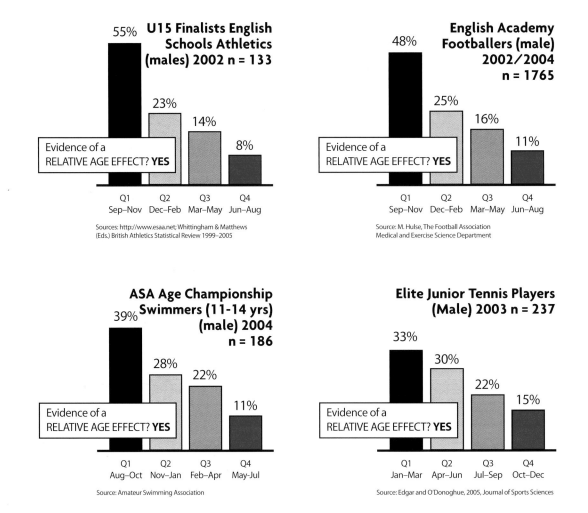

Figure 17: Relative age distribution in male squads for athletics, football, swimming and tennis (Morris and Nevill, 2007)

- The impact of relative age is important in much the same way as early and late maturation. The effects are early success, early selection for higher representative honours and continued participation. Performers not achieving early success can lose confidence. Research has shown those who are selected earlier receive more and better coaching, leading to a further widening of the gap. Several sports have recognised the problem and have taken different measures to try address it. One method is to 'age up' (also known as age on date) young performers on their actual birthday, rather than at the end of the year. Thus, the performer born at the beginning of the year is not competing with one born at the end of the year. Other solutions include increasing age bandings to six months rather than 12, or holding age group competitions (much easier in individual sports) several times a year.

- In terms of working with young performers, coaches should be aware of the basis on which they select young developing performers and ensure they are well informed of maturation levels and actual birth dates.

The conclusion of Chapter 2 drew attention to the difficulties of making selections based on comparisons of physiological capabilities and skill levels in young performers. The effects of early and late maturation and relative age should also be considered.

4. Phases of Growth and Measurement

This section highlights the key issues of growth and maturation at the different phases of growth in young people. Chapter 2 has already outlined the stages, so this section will expand on aforementioned information, highlighting the windows of trainability mentioned throughout Chapter 3.

Figure 18, adapted from Williams (2007) (see further reading for Chapter 2), illustrates the curve of speed of growth. It identifies six phases where growth rate of performers can be measured and monitored through infancy to adulthood.

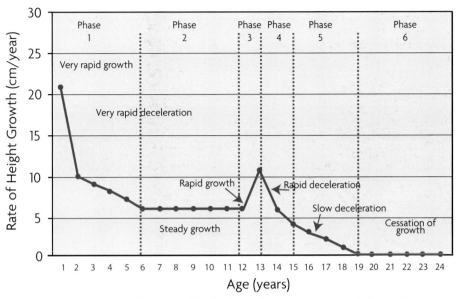

Figure 18: The six phases for the measurement of growth

Phase 1: Age 0 to 5/6

This phase is characterised by rapid growth during infancy and rapid deceleration of growth after the age of two. It is suggested measurement of standing height and weight is carried out every birthday.

Phase 2: Age 6 to the Onset of PHV

This phase is characterised by steady growth (on average 5–6cm per year). It is suggested measurement of standing, sitting height and arm span is carried out every birthday. If measurements are taken in a sports environment, the first one should occur at the beginning of the annual season. When the onset of PHV is identified, measurements of standing height should be taken every three months (quarterly).

During this period, the skill, speed and suppleness windows should be identified by chronological age.

Phase 3: From the Onset of PHV to PHV

This phase is characterised by rapid growth. In the first year of the onset of PHV, average growth is 6cm and 7cm for girls and boys respectively. In the second year, the average growth is 8cm and 9cm respectively. It is suggested measurement of standing height, sitting height and arm span is taken every three months, to monitor which part of the body is growing the fastest. A change in the centre of gravity, leg length and arm span will help the coach understand what is happening more easily. For example, when the performer is losing coordination and speed due to rapid growth.

During this phase, the aerobic window should be identified by the onset of PHV and the second speed window by chronological age. Coaches need to be aware of early, average and late maturers (see 'Early and Late Maturation' in this chapter).

Phase 4: From PHV Peak to Slow Deceleration

This phase is characterised by rapid deceleration in growth of about 7cm in boys and 6cm in girls in the first year after the peak, and 3cm in boys and 2cm in girls in the next year (Tanner, 1989). It is suggested measurement of standing height, sitting height and arm span is taken every three months to monitor deceleration.

During this period, the windows of aerobic power and strength can be identified after deceleration. That is to say, aerobic power should be trained after PHV. In terms of strength training for females, this can commence immediately after PHV or at the onset of menarche. For males, strength training can begin 12–18 months after PHV.

Phase 5: From Slow Deceleration of Growth to Cessation of Growth

Slow deceleration will start 2–3 years after PHV and will end with cessation of growth (Tanner, 1989).

The strength window should be identified, as described in Phase 4, and training loads and intensities gradually determined and progressed through analysis of the individual. All systems are now fully trainable.

Phase 6: Cessation of Growth

During this phase, individual analysis of the strengths and weaknesses of the performer will determine training loads and intensities.

Monitoring the phases of growth of biological markers (see Chapter 3, Figure 14) by the described measurements should inform the coach of when to optimise specific training for the young developing performer. In this way, training should take advantage of the opportunities provided by the sensitive periods of accelerated adaptation to training. Figure 19 provides a generic outline of trainability (Stafford 2005).

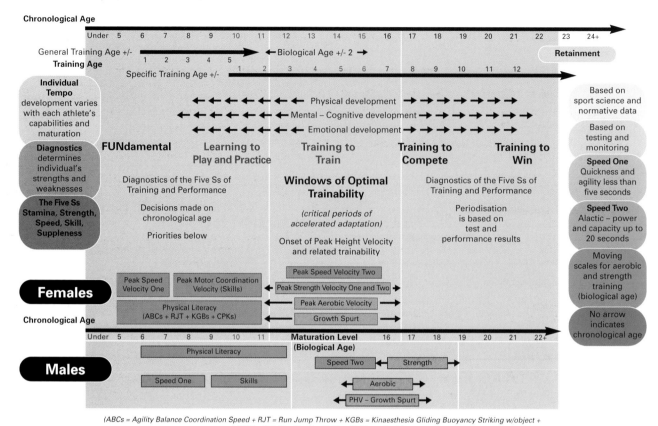

(ABCs = Agility Balance Coordination Speed + RJT = Run Jump Throw + KGBs = Kinaesthesia Gliding Buoyancy Striking w/object +
CPKs = Catching Passing Kicking Striking w/body)

Figure 19: Adaptation to training and optimal trainability (adapted from Balyi and Way, 2002 in Stafford, 2005)

Note: The arrows indicate moving scales for biological maturity (not chronological age) in relation to the onset of PHV.

This diagram identifies the:

- various windows of trainability, showing chronological age, general and sport-specific training age
- five stages of long-term athlete development
- moving scales of aerobic and strength trainability during the maturation period.

Before the onset of PHV and after maturation (post-puberty), simple analysis and testing can determine training priorities. This process needs to consider the windows of accelerated adaptation to training, and the requirements of the particular sport.

During and immediately after PHV, the pattern of growth should act as a guide to the type of training programme utilised. In this key phase, the annual periodised plan needs to take account of individual patterns of growth, so relevant windows of trainability (namely endurance, the second speed window and strength) can be fully exploited.

After maturation, analysis will again identify training priorities, by highlighting performer strengths and weaknesses. Training/competition and recovery programme design will be based on individual specific needs and the demands of the sport.

This generic information can easily be adjusted to sport-specific norms and demands.

Key Concepts and Summary

Monitoring Phases of Growth Prior to the Onset of PHV (Phases 1 and 2)

- FUNdamental movement and FUNdamental sports skills should be fully developed before the onset of PHV (ie a wide variety of movement and skill development sessions should be coached within a fun and game-related environment).
- Speed training should be an integral part of all-year-round physical activity and training, with special emphasis on speed, agility and quickness (eg less than five seconds of effort, focusing with full recovery) for boys 7–9 years and girls 6–8 years.
- Suppleness: the window of optimal trainability for flexibility for both genders occurs between the ages 6 and 10.
- Endurance and strength should be trained before the onset of PHV, but are not a high priority during this phase.
- In non-weight-bearing sports (such as swimming), a combination of endurance (aerobic capacity) and skill training is recommended.

Between the Onset of PHV and PHV Itself (Phase 3)

- Developing endurance and establishing an aerobic base should be a priority for late specialisation sports. This should be done specific to the sport.

- Development of the aerobic base in early specialisation sports should be determined by sport and event specificity.

- Development of skills and flexibility should be carefully monitored and maintained.

- Due to rapid growth during this period, non-weight-bearing aerobic activities are recommended for fitness training when necessary (ie to avoid conditions such as Osgood Schlatter's).

- Speed training should be trained all-year-round, regardless of the phase of the annual cycle. Special emphasis should be placed on the second speed window (ie 5–20 seconds' work), starting for girls at 11 years of age and boys at 13 years of age.

- Specific speed development period(s) should be identified in the annual periodised plan for block loading of speed training (ie during the specific preparatory, pre-competitive and competitive phases).

- Strength training should continue using medicine balls, Swiss balls and own body-weight exercises. Weightlifting techniques (ie free weight and Olympic lifting) should be introduced at the end of this phase, in preparation for the strength window post PHV.

Post PHV (Phase 4)

- Aerobic power training or interval training should be introduced in late specialisation sports after growth decelerates.

- After growth deceleration, the proper technique of free-weight training should be introduced to performers, so they will be ready to undertake strength and power training. This is very important from an injury prevention point of view.

- The strength windows of trainability:

  for females:
  - immediately after PHV
  - with the onset of menarche

  for males
  - 12–18 months after PHV.

Post PHV (Phases 5 and 6)

- After maturation, laboratory, field and performance tests will identify strengths and weaknesses of performers (for further information see Pankhurst, 2007). Periodised programmes should be designed considering strength and weaknesses in stamina, strength, speed, skill and suppleness. Short- and long-term planning strategies should be implemented on an individual basis.

5. Conclusion

This chapter has examined several key issues that will concern coaches wanting to develop quality training and competition programmes for young performers. The questions raised by early and late maturation and by the relative age effect, are important in that they could ultimately decide whether young performers remain in sport and/or reach their potential.

Good coaches will be aware of all the issues raised in this chapter and take them into account in their planning, training and competitive processes.

References

Bompa T. (1985) 'Talent identification', *Sports Science Periodical on Research and Technology in Sport*, GN-1, February: 1–11.

Bompa, T. (2000) *Total Training for Young Champions*. Champaign, Illinois: Human Kinetics. ISBN: 978-0736002-12-7.

Borms, J. (1986) 'The child and exercise: an overview,' *Journal of Sport Sciences*, 4: 3–20.

Canadian Sport for Life (2005) 'Long-term Athlete Development resource paper v2,' Canadian Sport for Life. ISBN: 0-9738274-0-8.

Morris, J.G. and Nevill, M.E. (2007) A sporting chance – enhancing opportunities for high-level sporting performance: influence of relative age. Loughborough University.

Pankhurst, A. (2007) *Planning and Periodisation*. Leeds: Coachwise Business Solutions/The National Coaching Foundation. ISBN: 978-1-905540-43-3.

Stafford, I. (2005) *Coaching for Long-term Athlete Development: to improve participation and performance in sport*. Leeds: Coachwise Business Solutions/The National Coaching Foundation. ISBN: 978-1-902523-70-5.

Tanner, J.M. (1989) *Foetus into Man: Physical Growth from Conception to Maturity*. Hertfordshire: Castlemead Publications. ISBN: 978-0-948555-24-4.

Further Reading

Bunker, D., Thorpe, R. and Almond, L. (1986) *Rethinking Games Teaching*. Loughborough: Loughborough University.

Dick, F. (2007) *Sports Training Principles*. London: A & C Black Publishers Ltd. ISBN: 978-0-713682-78-6.

Chapter 5: Growth and Maturation in Practice – Case Studies from Women's Football and Tennis

Brent Hills, Dawn Scott, Misia Gervis and Anne Pankhurst

Introduction

This chapter consists of two case studies: one from women's football, the other from tennis. Both are late specialisation sports; however, women's football highlights the complexities of a team sport and tennis reflects individual demands. The studies show how the sports incorporate the processes and complexities of growth, development and maturation in the planning of quality and relevant programmes, for the first three stages of long-term player development (LTPD).

CASE STUDY 1

The Impact of Growth and Maturation on Programme Planning for the Developmental Player

Women's Football – The First Three Stages

Brent Hills, Assistant National Coach, Women's Football, The Football Association

Dawn Scott, Exercise Scientist, The Football Association

Misia Gervis, Consultant Sports Psychologist, The Football Association and Brunel University

This case study is based on the:

- LTPD model for women's and girls' football, as created by The Football Association

- *Introductory Guide to Women's and Girls' Football*, published by The FA, 2006.

Throughout the first three stages of the LTPD pathway – FUNdamentals, Learning to Play and Practice and Training to Train – it is essential coaches, teachers and others involved in the development of young female players, are familiar with the principles and processes of growth, development and maturation. The sensitive windows of trainability referred to in Chapter 3, together with the technical, tactical, psychological, social and emotional development of young female players, must be taken into account in the planning of development pathways.

The Demands of Football

Football is a fast-moving game that, at adult level, requires players to use both aerobic and anaerobic energy systems at different times in the game both on and off the ball. The players will need high levels of balance, coordination, agility and movement to run and change direction quickly, while controlling, passing and receiving the ball, or defending against an opponent. Players need fast reactions, a high level of technical skill, speed, endurance and flexibility.

Stage 1 – FUNdamentals

The objective of this stage is to develop fundamental movement skills at age 6–9 years (for females).

The Philosophy of Coaching Football at this Stage

- Young female players should practise and master a wide range of fundamental movement skills before being introduced to football and other sport-specific skills.

- The game should be the teacher. Whenever appropriate, coaches and teachers should teach through the game and foster an atmosphere of freedom and fun (see Bunker et al, 1986).

- The ethos should be one of striving to win. However, winning at all costs is counterproductive. Most young people want to win when they play, so coaches need neither to encourage nor discourage this desire, but they do need to keep winning in perspective in the overall player development system.

- Creating a Stimulating Learning Environment (SLE) should be paramount in the planning process for coaches and teachers.

- As players respond to practice, repetition is important in fostering a love of technical mastery. Young players should be encouraged to practise outside the formal practice session.

- Coaches and teachers should use creative planning to achieve multiple outcomes (developing technical, tactical, mental and physical skills at the same time) throughout practice sessions.

- Ball manipulation and mastery is a worthwhile achievement within SLE.

- Practices for this stage should involve simple decision making by players.

- Each player should play in a variety of positions, including goalkeeper.

- Emphasis should be on developing the fundamental movement skills listed later in this case study.

- The first window of speed training (agility and quickness) that occurs during this stage of development should be exploited.

- Speed and endurance can be developed using fun games and activities.

- In order to develop all-round physical literacy at this stage, participation in as many sports and movement activities as possible should be encouraged.

- Basic rules and the historical ethics of sport can be introduced.

- Integration of the different factors of performance is a major objective at all stages of LTPD. Therefore, technical work for the FUNdamental stage, involving associated fundamental movement patterns, should be based on the specific themes, as listed in this case study.

Periodisation

Periodisation is not a factor during the FUNdamental stage. Instead, the overall physical activity programme of each player should be maximised, monitored and structured, in an appropriate social environment, to take advantage of every opportunity. Four or five sessions of physical activity per week are recommended, with at least two of these being football, if this is the preferred sport.

Training to Competition Ratios

Young players should be free to choose to compete with each other at any time during informal competition. Freedom and fun should always be driving philosophies in activities. If formal competitions are organised for the stage, they should be limited to 20 events per season/year.

The 10 Ss of Training and Performance During the FUNdamental Stage

The 10 Ss of training and performance are used as a basis for describing the first three LTPD stages throughout this case study.

- stamina
- strength
- speed
- skill
- suppleness
- structure/stature
- (p)sychology
- sustenance
- schooling
- sociocultural.

Stamina

Younger players are less efficient in many capacities than older players. They have lower levels of muscle power and smaller muscle energy stores. Consequently, they are at a disadvantage in terms of endurance capability. Therefore, any exposure to endurance training before the onset of puberty should be minimal and carefully planned. It is most likely that exposing players to warm-ups and small-sided games is more than enough to stimulate the aerobic system prior to puberty.

Strength

Strength can be defined as the ability to apply force against a resistance; strength enhances the performance and execution of many football skills. Furthermore, a well-designed strength-training programme will enable players to cope better with the physical stresses of training and competition.

Strength gains are possible in this stage, but are the result of improvements in motor coordination and neurological adaptations (see Chapter 3), rather than strength training itself. Technique work using the player's own body weight should be introduced at this age. Using a light, wooden pole or stick, players can be taught the movement patterns of some basic strength exercises, such as squats, lunges, pulls and cleans. In addition, light medicine ball work and Swiss ball exercises, taught with good technique in a fun way, can develop all-round improvements in coordination, dynamic strength and core stability.

Speed

Viru et al (1998) identified two windows of trainability for speed training in females: one at 6–8 and the other at 11–13 years of age (see Chapter 3).

In the FUNdamental stage, speed development is multidirectional and over a time frame of up to 5 seconds. Relatively small numbers of repetitions (six maximum in two sets) can be used. A ball should be included wherever possible. Speed training can be included in every session towards the end of the warm-up, when fatigue is not a factor. The ideal work:rest ratio ranges from 1:6 to 1:8, with at least three minutes' recovery between sets.

Skill

The emphasis at this stage should be on developing the fundamental movement skills of:

- ABCs – agility, balance, coordination and speed

- RJT – running, jumping and throwing

- KGB – kinaesthetics, gliding, buoyancy and striking with body parts

- CPK – catching, passing and kicking, and striking with an implement.

In order to develop all-round physical literacy, participation in as many sports and movement activities as possible should be encouraged. The ability to read the sporting environment (decision making) is also a component of physical literacy.

As highlighted above, the integration of different capacities is a major theme running through LTPD technical work. Therefore, practising of technical skills in football should take account of the following themes at this stage:

- core/individual skills – these techniques are basic to all players, if they are to master and enjoy the sport. They should be emphasised as the basic skills of football (eg ball manipulation exercises, juggling)

- receiving the ball

- passing less than 25m

- turning, dribbling and running with the ball

- heading (soft-touch ball)

- finishing goalscoring opportunities

- counter-attacking

- defending

- goalkeeping

- small-sided games (4 v 4 to 6 v 6).

The basic rules and ethics of the sport should be introduced.

Suppleness

The optimal window of trainability for flexibility is between 9 and 12 years of age, before the onset of puberty (see Chapter 3). The FUNdamental stage is, therefore, the ideal time to begin a general flexibility programme. Overall flexibility should be encouraged, as this will promote good, basic physical development.

Flexibility can be introduced through dynamic and fun activities at this level, and should be undertaken five to six times per week if improvement is required. Three sessions per week are adequate to maintain performance.

Structure/Stature

In Chapter 4, Figure 18 showed the velocity of growth at different ages. The discussion in Chapters 2 and 4 has highlighted that, at the FUNdamental stage, growth in stature is more gradual than during puberty. Coaches need to understand the processes of growth, development and maturation described in Chapters 2, 3 and 4, and also be aware of different growth patterns between players.

(P)sychology

Working with young players requires coaches to take a number of key elements into account from a psychological perspective. Young developing players need to feel secure and valued in their playing environment. They find it difficult to learn when they are uncomfortable and anxious. Every child should feel part of the group and be able to make friends. Being with friends is a key reason why young people remain involved in sport. The coach's role in facilitating this process is significant.

Firstly, positive feedback from coaches and other adults is essential for young players. Secondly, effort, as well as outcome and ability, should be rewarded, as this encourages players to keep trying things, even when they find them difficult at the first attempt. Children, unlike adults, are still developing cognitive abilities. So, for example, judging the speed and flight of the ball is a complex cognitive skill which very young players find difficult. Coaches should have a good understanding of the capabilities of young people, so they understand how they impact on the performance of certain skills, and how they can be developed. Success leads to confidence, so opportunities should be maximised for young players to be successful.

An effective coach will understand how young players learn. Sometimes, the reason that a child doesn't understand what is required is because it is not presented in the appropriate learning style. The majority of young players learn visually and kinaesthetically, so helping young players learn skills through demonstration and visualisation can be very effective. When introducing new skills, ask players to **imagine** themselves doing the skill, as well as actually performing it. This will help the process of integrating psychological skills into physical practice and can help enhance learning.

Sustenance

• Nutrition and Hydration

Players should be encouraged to develop good nutritional habits at an early age. Information and the example of good role models (such as the coach or older players) may help young players develop sound, everyday eating habits, as well as specific preparation for games. At the FUNdamental stage, parents will notice a decrease in their child's rate of growth, and possibly a change in appetite. Children may change the amount of food they eat at each meal, refuse to eat meats and vegetables, or want to eat the same foods day after day. The role of the parents is vital in providing optimum nutrition to the growing child. Parent education should help develop an understanding that the nutritional needs of a growing, active child cannot be based on scaled down adult recommendations. Depending on the stage of growth of the player, parents should be encouraged to understand the following:

- children should consistently eat three balanced meals per day, with two or three small, healthy snacks between meals

- a high calcium intake is essential to support bone accretion

- during sub-maximal exercise, children utilise more fat, but less carbohydrate

- children drink only when they are thirsty and this is too late, since they are already dehydrated

- hydration in young players should be closely monitored. Dehydration seems to be more detrimental to children than it does to adults (Bar-Or, 2000).

• Rest

The recommendation for this, and every age group, is 8–10 hours of sleep per 24 hours. Maintenance of a regular sleep schedule and an optimal sleeping environment for young players is very important.

• Recovery – regeneration

The coach is always trying to achieve maximum adaptation to training by balancing training loads with appropriate recovery for individual players (see Chapter 3). The strategies, which the coach should attempt to employ and teach to young players, are:

- warm-up

- cool-down

- hydration

- nutrition

- sleep

- rest and relaxation.

Schooling

Coaches must bear in mind that school-based activities also form part of the individual's weekly physical workload. A daily session of sport and exercise is beneficial to young people.

Therefore, all activities should be coordinated to ensure variety, the development of fundamental movement skills and the avoidance of overtraining. Training and competition should not interfere with school, academic and other activities.

Sociocultural

The following key factors should be considered when working with young players:

- **lifestyle** – good hygiene, eating and sleeping habits should be established during this stage

- **socialisation via sport** – the general values and norms of society, such as fairness and respect for others, are important and can be taught to, and learnt by, young players in sport

- **sport socialisation** – sport-specific values, norms and behaviours are important in any sport. Young players need to learn the subculture of football in order to contribute to the sport in a positive way.

Stage 2 – Learning to Play and Practice

The objective of this stage is to develop fundamental sports skills, including football skills, in females aged 8–11.

In this age range, players will begin to play an increasing number of formal football matches. These will be for a club or the school, but should remain developmental in their ethos. Competitive programmes that become results driven will not enhance the enjoyment or experience of players, and can lead to early drop out. While early maturers often stand out during childhood, research (and experience) suggests it is the late maturers who have a greater potential to reach and maintain elite levels of performance in the long term. Later maturers will benefit greatly from spending longer on the activities suggested for this stage.

The Philosophy of Coaching Football at this Stage

- The atmosphere in practice sessions should still revolve around freedom and fun.

- The ethos should be one of striving to win. Winning at all costs is counterproductive.

Wanting to win is quite normal (and desirable) with young players. The coach's role, therefore, is to keep winning in perspective during this stage of development.

- The ages of 8–11 for girls coincides with peak motor coordination development (see Chapter 3). This stage is often referred to as the golden age of skill learning. Coaches should focus on technique and skill development whenever possible. This also includes the physical and psychological components of learning.

- Players can be introduced to general physical conditioning at the awareness level, but integrating physical conditioning with technical work is more important.

- The whole programme should be holistic in nature, in seeking to influence all aspects of player development.

Periodisation

Periodisation at this stage should be double periodisation. Therefore, there should be two macrocycles in the year.

- Macrocycle 1 with the first preparation and competition period is from July to November.

- Macrocycle 2 with the second preparation and competition period is from February to April.

- December and January are a reconditioning mid-winter break without formal competition.

- Participation in alternate team and individual sports is important during May and June.

Furthermore, overall technical and athletic development is a key focus. The longer the preparation period, the higher, more consistent and competent competitive performances will be. An increase in the length of preparation phases, with a mid-winter reconditioning phase, will ensure peaks are higher and sustained for longer in competition. The length of the competition phase ensures players do not overplay. There is adequate time to develop, prepare and recuperate.

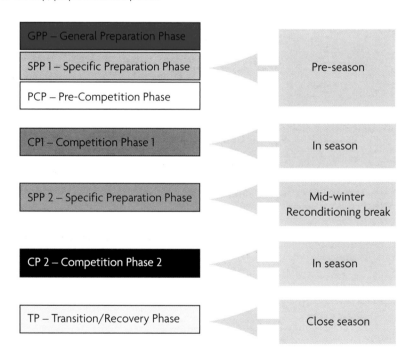

Figure 20: Periodised annual plan (adapted from The FA)

Ancillary capacities including warm-up, cool-down, stretching, nutrition, hydration, recovery and regeneration, basic mental preparation, taper and peaking for competition, and pre- and post-competition routines, should all be introduced at this stage. Such factors are further developed as players progress through the development pathway.

Fundamental movement skills and a variety of sport-specific movement skills should be developed to ensure players continue to develop physical literacy.

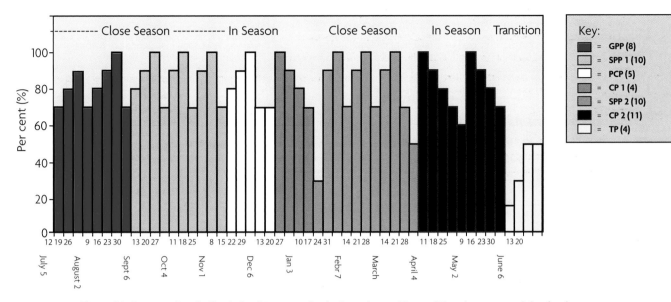

Figure 21: An annual periodised plan for a team in the Learning to Play and Practice stage training load (volume + intensity)

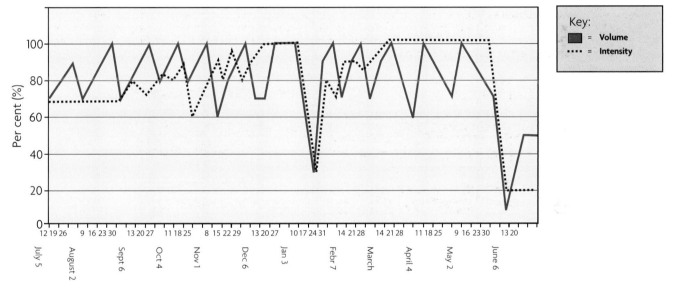

Figure 22: An annual periodised plan for a team in the Learning to Play and Practice stage training load (volume and intensity)

Note: These are sample plans which should be adjusted to suit the individual needs of the team.

The annual double periodised plan is shown in Figure 21.

The first macrocycle of the plan consists of:

- 8 microcycles (weeks) – general preparation phase (GPP)
- 10 microcycles – specific preparation phase (SPP1)
- 5 microcycles – pre-competitive phase (PCP)
- a short 4 microcycles – competitive phase (CP1)
- 1 week – rest.

The second macrocycle consists of:

- 10 microcycles – specific preparatory phase (SPP2)
- 11 microcycles – competitive phase (CP2)
- 4 weeks – transition phase (TP), passive and active rest.

It is important to note the long duration of the specific preparation phase in each macrocycle provides time for learning technical and decision-making skills, thus exploiting the opportunity provided by the skill-hungry years.

Figure 22 shows the volume and intensity of training at different stages in each of the microcycles shown in Figure 21. Volume and intensity are important because they enable the player to reach both the microcycle goals and those for the annual plan.

Figures 21 and 22 were designed by LTPD experts and FA national coaches. They allow young female players to adequately, and scientifically, prepare to compete with higher quality players.

Training to Competition Ratios

In the Learning to Play and Practice stage, it is recommended that no more than 20 competitive games in a formal setting are played in a year, to avoid overplay and psychological burnout. Four to five hours per week can be given to general sports participation, with two hours per week being given to football-specific activities. One to two hours per week can be devoted to introductory physical conditioning, although integrating these into other sporting activities will prove more efficient.

The 10 Ss of Training and Performance During the Learning to Play and Practice Stage

This stage has already been highlighted as the golden age of learning. This means overall emphasis should be on motor skill development. Stamina, strength, speed and suppleness should be developed further. If possible within a football context, the principle of multiple outcomes will result in training sessions becoming more effective and efficient. The football programme should take account of training, competition and recovery for each individual, in order to optimise development and performance.

Wilf Paish (1991) devised a formula for splitting practice sessions into training units. Each unit gives an adequate amount of time for individual physical and technical capabilities to be developed (strength, speed, agility, balance, coordination, suppleness, stamina and skills). This formula can be adapted to take account of the windows of trainability and to give more time in each unit to the capabilities that will be developed optimally, at the individual player's stage of growth, development and maturation.

The following formula can be used:

1. Decide the relative importance of the different factors (eg skills need 50% of total training time at the Learning to Play and Practice stage).

2. Divide the total minutes of training time available by 10 (eg three training sessions of one hour give 180 minutes of training time. Thus, in this example, each unit is 18 minutes).

3. If skills require 50% or five units of training time, 90 minutes should be allocated to skills.

	FUNdamentals	L2PP	T2T
Strength	1	1	2
Speed and ABC	2	2	1 (2)
Suppleness	1	1	2
Stamina	1	1	1 (2)
Skill	5	5	4

Figure 23: Unit totals for the different capacities for FUNdamentals, Learning to Play and Practice and Training to Train stages of development

As has been highlighted already in this case study, coaches should strive for multiple outcomes from each activity, in order to maximise training time and because sport is about integrating all the factors of performance. Coaches should, therefore, design practices that incorporate technical outcomes. They should also work, for example, on stamina, because this is a more efficient use of time. The physical skills in Figure 23 for the FUNdamentals, Learning to Play and Practice, and Training to Train stages should be integrated with technical/tactical work where possible.

Stamina

Developing stamina at the Learning to Play and Practice stage is similar to the training undertaken at the FUNdamentals stage. It should be adequate, carefully planned and maintained through warm-ups, fun activities and skill circuits, such as corridor and figure-of-eight practices.

Strength

Strength is a fundamental component of every movement a football player performs while on the field of play. When trained with close attention to the correct technique, the risk of injury is very low. Strength training itself will help prevent injury. Technique work should be continued at this stage, using the player's own body weight, medicine and Swiss balls, with exercises based on fun, multiple outcomes. The use of a light wooden pole or stick can also be continued. Slow progressions in hopping and jumping activities, combined with technical strength training, can also be utilised.

As described in the FUNdamentals stage, strength gains are possible, but are the result of improvements in motor coordination and neurological adaptations. The intention should be to ensure the improvement of coordination, dynamic strength and core stability.

Speed

In principle, players at this stage are between the two windows of trainability. However, speed training should be continued, following the same parameters as at the FUNdamentals stage. That is, it should be multidirectional and up to five seconds with a small number of repetitions (six maximum x two sets). The football can be included whenever possible.

Speed training should be undertaken towards the end of the warm-up, when players are not tired. The work:rest ratio should be 1:6 to 1:8, with at least three minutes' recovery between sets.

Skill

Fundamental motor coordination skills should be developed, in girls, between the ages of 8–11, if they are to reach their optimum level of performance in future years. If this skill window is missed, a carefully planned remedial programme can make up some, but not all, of the deficit.

Technical/tactical skills at this stage will include:

- core/individual skills – these techniques are fundamental to all players if they are to master and enjoy the sport. They should be emphasised as the basic skills of football (eg ball manipulation exercises and juggling)
- receiving the ball
- passing up to 25m
- individual attacking moves (turning, dribbling, running with the ball)
- heading (soft-touch ball)
- finishing goalscoring opportunities
- combination plays
- counter-attacking
- defending
- goalkeeping
- small-sided games (4 v 4 to 7 v 7).

Suppleness

The window of optimal trainability for suppleness (flexibility) is between 9 and 12 years of age. Therefore, this can be introduced through dynamic and fun activities at both the FUNdamental and Learning to Play and Practice stages, with five to six training sessions per week, if improvement is required. Three sessions per week is adequate to maintain performance. For early maturers, flexibility training is important and should become more of a focus.

Structure/Stature

At the Learning to Play and Practice stage, a number of early developers will be approaching, or be experiencing, the onset of PHV. Therefore, monitoring for PHV should be well-organised and more regular for these players. The FA recommends measurements be taken every three months to accurately determine the growth spurt of individual players.

(P)sychology

Between the ages of 8 and 11, players are still developing their cognitive abilities. This is important to recognise, as cognitive ability impacts on a number of key areas, including decision making, attentional control, tracking and perceptual awareness. Coaches must consider the possibility that a player who is unable to perform a particular skill set, might not be cognitively ready to do so.

From a social psychology perspective, research shows girls need to feel accepted and part of the group. Often, they will only become involved in football if their friends do. Therefore, the coach should maximise opportunities to integrate players and enhance friendships, through good social support structures that help players feel comfortable.

Between 8 and 11, young players begin to link effort to success, learning that the harder they try, the more likely it is they will succeed. Between 7–9 years of age, there is limited understanding of this concept. In addition, adult perception of effort, and that of a child's, can be very different. Coaches should consider what a child understands by being asked to 'try harder'.

The use of imagery, as a problem-solving tool for this age group, can help maximise positive outcomes. Players should be encouraged to imagine themselves being successful. Coaches should try to get them to recreate such performances in as much detail as possible, building time into sessions for this. This will help enhance the self-efficacy of young players. The more positive successful outcomes players achieve, the stronger their self-efficacy.

Sustenance

• Nutrition and Hydration

The process of educating players and parents about good habits of nutrition and hydration should be a continual one. As players grow older, they are more able to understand the links between good dietary habits and their ability to play and practise well. Players may change the amount of food they eat at each meal time and decide they no longer like certain foods. This is part of growing up. The role of parents is important, since they are the prime agents looking after young players of this age. Therefore, parental education continues to be important.

Coaches and parents should bear in mind the following issues:

– Young people should consistently eat three balanced meals per day, with two or three small, healthy snacks between meals.

– Young people need greater protein intake, to satisfy growth requirements.

– A high calcium intake is essential to support bone accretion.

– Some girls who take part in sport may need additional iron.

– During sub-maximal exercise, children utilise more fat, but less carbohydrate.

– Hydration in young players should be closely monitored.

• Rest

The recommendation for this age group is 8–10 hours of sleep per 24 hours. Maintenance of a regular sleep schedule and an optimal sleeping environment for young players is very important.

• Recovery – regeneration

The guidelines described in the FUNdamentals stage should also be applied at this stage, with slightly more sophistication. In addition, and as players grow older, pool sessions and recovery strategies should be introduced. Online training diaries can be used to help players, and those involved in supporting them, monitor, organise and balance their lifestyles.

Schooling

At this stage, and certainly towards the age of 11 with the changes to secondary education, schoolwork becomes more important. The majority of girls tend to understand the significance of schoolwork. At the Learning to Play and Practice stage, the integration of all activities in each player's schedule is essential. Links between the different agencies (ie school, club and home) are important to avoid overplay, and to ensure a variety of activities.

Sociocultural

In addition to lifestyle, socialisation through sport and sport socialisation itself, team building and group dynamics should be important considerations for the coach. Girls at this stage prefer to play in teams and will enjoy football, but only if they are able to make friends and feel valued in the environment.

Stage 3 – Training to Train

The objective of this stage, for females aged 10–14, is to 'build the engine' for the future. This includes physical preparation and continuing development of football-specific and decision-making skills.

This is a crucial stage in the development of players. During this stage, and with maturation levels in mind, players will need to train endurance, speed and strength, in addition to ABC. They will also need to build a greater repertoire of football-related skills. As a result, some experts refer to this stage as 'building the engine'.

The Philosophy of Coaching Football at this Stage

• The atmosphere created in training should be one of understanding and developing skill.

• Creating a Stimulating Learning Environment (SLE) continues to be of paramount importance.

• Repetition is important to refine and develop technical and tactical excellence.

• Multiple outcomes from every session are important to maximise the use of training time. Specific work should be undertaken to address a particular need, should this be required.

• Ball manipulation skills and mastery continue to be a theme.

• As players mature, decision making takes on new and broader concepts.

• Players should continue to experience all positions, including goalkeeper. However, most will have settled on one or two positions by the end of this stage. It is recognised that maturation rates and genetic make-up can influence choice regarding final playing position(s). Late maturers may decide on a different position much later.

• At this stage of development, young talented players can be approached by a number of people to play for different organisations. However, with effective communication and a recognition that the interests of the player must be at the heart of any decisions, these issues can be resolved to ensure decisions are player-centred.

• Windows of accelerated adaptation for endurance and strength training at this stage should be emphasised.

• The second speed window should be developed at this stage.

Periodisation

At the Training to Train stage, double periodisation (two macrocycles) should be planned. The structure of this is as follows:

- Macrocycle 1 has the first preparation and competition period from July to November.

- Macrocycle 2 has the second preparation and competition period from February to April.

- A mid-winter break to suit player needs for reconditioning, technical/tactical work and to emphasise the ratio of competition to practice.

Within the periodised plan, warm-up and cool-down will play an added part in preparing and recovering from performance. Mental preparation, recovery and regeneration, and pre-, during and post-game routines should be introduced and developed. Tapering and peaking will become a factor in periodisation.

Careful monitoring of growth is of critical importance during this stage, and in the subsequent Training to Compete stages. As discussed in Chapter 4, players of the same chronological age can differ by as much as four years at this stage. This will affect technical/tactical, psychological, physical and social development. Coaches should be aware of the differences in biological maturity when attempting to assess players. Appropriate training should be introduced at the relevant maturation period. Continued emphasis on athletic development and technical mastery should form the mainstays of the programme.

While other sports continue to play an important role, both for variety and cross-training, balance begins to shift firmly in football's favour. At the Training to Train stage, the recommendation is for two sports, with football as the main one.

Figure 24 shows the training and competition load for a female football player at this stage.

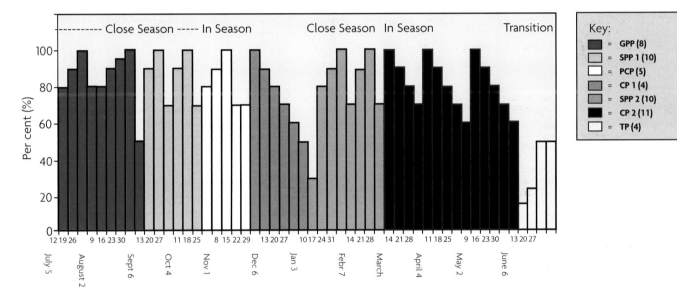

Figure 24: Annual periodised plan for a team in the Training to Train stage training load (volume + intensity)

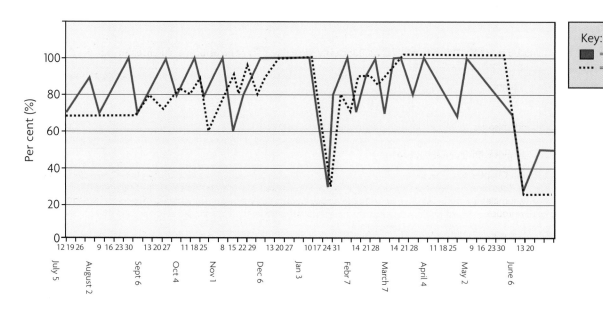

Figure 25: Annual periodised plan for a team in the Learning to Play and Practice stage training load (volume and intensity)

Note: These are sample plans which should be adjusted to suit the individual needs of the team.

The annual double periodised plan is shown in Figure 24.

The first macrocycle of the plan consists of:

- 9 microcycles (weeks) – general preparation phase (GPP)

- 6 microcycles – specific preparation phase (SPP1)

- 5 microcycles – pre-competitive phase (PCP)

- 6 microcycles – competitive phase (CP1)

- 1 week – rest.

The second macrocycle consists of:

- 8 microcycles – specific preparatory phase (SPP2)

- 14 microcycles – competitive phase (CP2)

- 4 weeks – transition phase (TP), passive and active rest.

Note the differences in the periodised plan between the Learning to Play and Practice and Training to Train stages. At this stage, competition is increased from 14 to 20 microcycles and the specific preparation microcycles are decreased from 21 to 14.

Figure 25 shows the volume and intensity of training at different stages, in each of the microcycles shown in Figure 24. This is important to enable the player to reach the goals for each microcycle, as well as for the annual plan.

Training to Competition Ratios

The maximum training to competition/practice ratio should be 3:1 or lower (4:1), if possible. This means one match to four or more practice sessions.

At this stage, it is recommended no more than 25 formal, competitive games are undertaken, to avoid overplay and psychological burnout.

Two to four hours per week can be given to general sports participation, with the same time allocated to football-specific activities. Two to five hours per week should be devoted to physical conditioning. However, integrating these hours into other sporting activities, where possible, is more efficient.

The 10 Ss of Training and Performance During the Training to Train Stage

Stamina

Scientific studies by Bangsbo et al (2007) and Rienzi et al (2000) clearly show that enhancing aerobic endurance can improve the performance of footballers. Aerobic endurance can be improved by increasing the:

- distance covered in training
- work intensity
- number of sprints and episodes, involving the ball, during practice.

Optimal aerobic training begins with the onset of PHV.

Onset of PHV (as outlined in Chapter 6) is, therefore, a marker for the accelerated adaptation of the aerobic system. This is known as peak aerobic velocity (PAV). The discussion on periodisation mentioned that, at this stage, biological maturity can vary by up to four years. When training aerobic capability, females aged 10–14 years can either be grouped according to biological maturation, or practices can be designed for mixed ability groups.

Non-weight-bearing aerobic activities (eg swimming and cycling) have a place in this stage of development, because they help avoid overuse injuries and psychological burnout.

Strength

Strength training has two windows of accelerated adaptation during the Training to Train stage. The first is immediately after PHV and the second begins with the onset of menarche: that is, between 1–1.5 years after PHV (see Chapter 3).

PHV will determine when resistance training programmes at this stage should start. In football, strength training with young players should only be undertaken with the supervision of qualified staff. The FA takes expert advice on this subject.

For females, strength performance levels off during puberty and does not visibly change thereafter. From puberty onwards, boys are significantly stronger than girls in the upper body and arms, but there is less difference in leg strength. In general, strength visibly relates to body size and fat-free muscle mass.

Olympic lifting techniques, progressing from working with a wooden pole at the earlier stages, should be comprehensively taught and learnt before weights are added. Such techniques should be taught in the Learning to Play and Practice stage, with little or no weight, in order to perfect for future work.

Speed

The second speed window (anaerobic alactic power) comes in the Training to Train stage (Chapter 3). This window occurs between the ages of 11–13 for females. Linear, lateral and multidirectional speed should be practised at intervals of between 5 and 20 seconds. Coaches familiar with speed training in earlier stages of player development will know that such training is best undertaken in the later part of the training session warm-up, when fatigue is not a factor. Speed training should be undertaken all-year-round.

Skill

This stage is characterised by the onset of PHV, which frequently results in players temporarily losing coordination as they grow rapidly. Therefore, coaches must be both patient and reassuring during this stage. They should also be wary of making decisions about future ability, based on performances during the growth spurt.

Individual technical and tactical work should be emphasised and continue to be improved while the player is moving through the growth spurt.

Technical/tactical training will include:

- core/individual skills – these techniques are fundamental to all players if they are to master and enjoy the sport. They should be emphasised as the basic skills of football (eg ball manipulation and juggling)
- receiving
- passing less than 30m
- individual attacking moves (turning, dribbling and running with the ball)
- heading (soft-touch ball)
- finishing goalscoring opportunities
- combination plays
- counter-attacking
- defending
- goalkeeping
- small-sided to full games (6 v 6 to 11 v 11).

Suppleness

As the player progresses and matures, flexibility training should continue. This allows the player to develop strength while adjusting to the changes that occur in the body. At some stage in the player's development, muscle tightness will become more prevalent. This is largely due to a delay in the muscle response as a result of the increasing length of bones. At this stage, an appropriate stretching and flexibility programme is vital, and should be in the form of static stretching or proprioceptive neuromuscular facilitation (PNF). This must be clearly explained and safely demonstrated to players. Dynamic mobility should always be used in preparation for practice and competition.

Structure/Stature

During this stage of player development, the body and its physical capabilities are developing rapidly, but at varying rates in different individuals. As has been discussed on several occasions, chronological age is not the most appropriate way to group players.

Training to Train is the most complex stage in LTPD for both player and coach. All trainable factors are influenced by the onset of PHV and, as such, they should be exploited during the most appropriate window of trainability. If players miss these windows, they will have fitness and skill deficits later, meaning they may never reach real genetic potential.

It is partly for this reason, and because of overplaying, that many players plateau during this stage. The resultant loss of motivation leads to many players dropping out from the sport at this early age.

According to Tanner (1989), the average increase in height for girls is 6cm in the first year and 8cm in the second year of the onset of PHV. Girls at this stage experience a growth in hip width. As a rule, leg length reaches its peak first and is 6–9 months ahead of any increase in trunk length. Shoulder and chest width are the last to reach their peaks. Peak muscle growth velocity (peak weight velocity) occurs 6–12 months after PHV. The onset of menarche (the first menstrual cycle) tends to occur just over a year after PHV (see Chapter 2).

(P)sychology

It is important at this stage that coaches:

- have realistic expectations of players
- remember at all times that players are young people first and players second.

It can be easy for coaches to be concerned with achievement and lose sight of what the players themselves want. Coaches need always to put players first and ensure the needs of the player, not the coach, are the determining factors in any decision making that takes place. An effective way to help coaches understand their players better could be the use of performance profiling. This process requires the input of the player. If done correctly, this can lead to a more effective goal-setting process, as long as the player is involved in developing and setting their own goals.

The most important issue is to ensure players receive constant positive reminders of their successes, however small these might be. This will help create confident players in the future. Players should be encouraged to use visualisation to remind them of aspects of their performance they did well.

Success in football is about the ability of players to work well as a team. It is important coaches create an open, trusting environment, where players feel safe in saying what they think and how they feel. This will help translate into game situations, where communication is paramount.

Sustenance

- **Nutrition and Hydration**

The links between hydration, nutrition and performance can be emphasised further at this stage of player development. Carefully prescribed nutritional supplements can be added during the growth spurt. Sports drinks can help rehydration after exercise, although many players will already be familiar with them.

The quality (nutrient content) and quantity (calories) of the diet should also be more closely monitored, to limit any unnecessary body fat gains. These are more likely as girls experience hormonal changes, menarche and increased body fat stores.

- **Rest**

The guidelines for adequate sleep and regularity of the sleep pattern, as described in the previous two stages, should also be applied here.

- **Recovery – regeneration**

The same principles that were applied in the first two stages of development continue to be important. At this stage, however, further techniques can be added, such as introduction to compression garments and cold-water immersion.

Training to Train is the most critical developmental stage because of the lasting effect it can have on an individual's sporting potential and health. During this stage, adolescents are exposed to increased training loads at the same time as they are experiencing rapid physical changes. Rapid growth, especially of muscle, bone and connective tissue, coupled with hormonal changes and an increase in mechanical loading, requires careful management. This is a very stressful time emotionally and socially, as most adolescents are studying hard to take career-determining exams, while experiencing increased social and psychological challenges from their peers and family.

More than any other developmental stage, this is the one that can expose the gifted player to overtraining, overuse injuries and burnout. It is very important for the coach and player to monitor individual adaptations, by keeping records of training loads, performances and player responses to these and other stresses.

Each player should also have a personalised training diary in which to keep this data. The FA has encouraged the use of training diaries in their licensed female centres of excellence, and is piloting the use of an online diary with a variety of players.

In addition to resting heart rate (RHR), body weight, quality of sleep and fatigue levels, the daily checklist should include ratings for hydration status (monitoring urine colour), self-esteem, muscle soreness, appetite, external stresses (home and school), illness or injury, and, for females, a record of the onset of each menstrual cycle, flow and pain, as well as any other symptoms. If a female has not started menstruation by the time she is 16, there are increased future health risks, so it is important she consults a suitably qualified medical specialist for advice.

This is also a critical time to develop medical and sports science screening and pre-season testing. In particular, musculoskeletal evaluations are critical to identify any of the common growth problems associated with the onset of PHV, especially those related to the spine and lower limbs.

Schooling

The key to sound development is often to keep a balanced perspective on all parts of everyday life. Therefore, careful monitoring of the daily schedule that allows time for all-important activities, in addition to sporting demands, is important. Incompatibility and overlap between different school sports and competitions should be avoided.

Sociocultural

The social relationships that develop between, for example, a right fullback, a right midfielder and a centre forward are important, and should be considered by coaches. Such relationships could be a determining factor in the progress each player makes, and their ultimate performance levels.

In the latter part of this stage, young players will be competing domestically and internationally. Some 14 year olds will have graduated to the under-15 international development pool. It is important to use these competitive experiences to promote the development of the whole person, and to encourage players to take an increasing responsibility for their own learning opportunities. This will help individuals become more adjusted and able to cope with a variety of situations later in life, whether in a sporting, social or work arena. It is all too easy to forget to 'put the ball away'.

This case study of the first three stages of the player development pathway for women's football has been comprehensive in discussing all the important aspects of each stage. The principles remain the same for all three stages, but the detail for training and competition at each stage will change as the player grows and matures. This case study, therefore, has important information for every coach. When this detail is applied to programmes for young female footballers on an individual basis, the opportunity for each of them to reach whatever potential they have is increased immeasurably.

CASE STUDY 2

The Impact of Growth and Maturation on Programme Planning for the Developmental Player

Tennis – The First Three Stages

Istvan Balyi and Anne Pankhurst

This case study is based on:

- a long-term player development (LTPD) model for tennis, created by a group of expert coaches within the sport
- a published chapter in the International Tennis Federation's *Strength and Conditioning for Tennis* (2003) entitled 'Long-term Athlete Development, Trainability and Physical Preparation of Tennis Players'
- coaching experience with developmental players in the UK and the USA.

The case study details the progression, by both male and female players, through the first three stages of the LTPD pathway in an individual late specialisation sport. In principle, these three stages determine the ultimate performance levels of a tennis player. Growth, development and maturation, the windows of trainability and technical, tactical, physical and mental preparation, are integrated during the first three stages. The process and activities described could be used by other individual sports, provided that sport-specific needs are taken into consideration.

The Demands of Tennis

Tennis is a game that requires the use of both aerobic and anaerobic energy systems. At the adult level, a match can last for an indeterminate time (typically between 1.5–4 hours) and the outcome is not known until the final point is completed. In addition, the sport can be played on a variety of surfaces, from slow red clay to a very fast grass court. Play can be indoors or outdoors. Tennis requires high levels of fitness, technical and tactical expertise, and mental/emotional control. It is an open skill sport that requires tactical understanding and decision making at a high level, as well as the performance of technical skills, all of which are improved as players reach puberty and eventual maturation.

Stage 1 – FUNdamentals

The objective of this stage is to develop fundamental movement skills between the ages of 6–8 for females and 6–9 for males.

The Philosophy of Coaching Tennis at this Stage

As highlighted in Chapter 3, fundamental movement skills should be coached, practised and mastered before sport-specific skills are introduced. These fundamental skills underpin those of all sports. During this stage, activities should be well structured and fun. Emphasis is on the quality development of players' physical capabilities and fundamental movement skills. The coach's attention to detail is paramount, to ensure young players learn skills to the highest level. The development of the young player as a 'whole' person is an important consideration.

Time should be allocated in each and every coaching session for children to practise fundamental movement skills. The development of these, using a positive and fun approach, is essential for future athletic performance.

The use of correctly sized equipment, relevant sized playing areas and modified scoring systems is also crucial if young players are to progress and enjoy the sport.

Participation in a wide range of sports is encouraged for at least two reasons:

1. A variety of sports will help young players physically and mentally, and will avoid early burnout.

2. Other sports will contribute to the movement skill base young players need, namely agility, balance and coordination, as well as providing social interaction.

Planned training, competition and recovery time will ensure improved adaptation will take place. This, in turn, will lead to better long-term sport-specific development.

Periodisation

Formal periodisation is not appropriate during the FUNdamentals stage. However, all training programmes should be structured and monitored. For the majority of tennis players, activities are based around the school year. During school holidays, many young players take part in tennis-based fun events and camps, as well as other sports and activities.

If tennis is the preferred sport, participation two or three times a week is recommended. Participation in other sports and activities, three or four times a week, is also important for future excellence. If players decide at a later stage to leave the sport, the skills they have acquired during the FUNdamentals stage will be of benefit in other sports and recreational activities. In the long term, their quality of life, health and well-being will be enhanced.

Training to Competition Ratios

There is no precise training to competition ratio at this stage. It is recommended young players experience more fun training activities than formal competition. Competitive skills can be learnt within training sessions, in game-based activities and in team competition that teaches the essence of winning and losing, and rules and scoring. Young players, especially girls, should play on intra- and inter-club teams in time-based competition. Scoring methods and types of competition should be adapted to suit young children. Young players can compete in teams whenever there is an appropriate opportunity.

While the framework of the five Ss of training and performance, as described in Chapter 3, is an important feature of the players' programme at this stage, there are additional factors. The 10 Ss of training and performance that were used in the football case study are also applicable to tennis.

The 10 Ss of Training and Performance During the FUNdamentals Stage

Stamina

Coaches should understand that at this stage, trainability of the aerobic system is good. In principle, the aerobic system is always trainable and, before the onset of PHV, healthy, active kids are 'aerobic machines' (Bar-Or, 1996). Aerobic training should be in the form of activities with an aerobic component. Young players can have a short attention span, so activities should be changed frequently to ensure interest. Aerobic activities on and off court should be emphasised. Ultra-short interval training relays and shuttle runs could be used to develop endurance during this stage.

Strength

Strength gains in pre-puberty are possible, although, as discussed previously for this age group, they are mainly in relative strength (percentage improvements) rather than in absolute strength. At this stage, strength gains occur through improvements in motor coordination and morphological and neurological development and adaptations. Exercise and increased muscle activation will also improve strength. Coaches will know that structural changes, such as muscle hypertrophy, should not be expected for this age group.

Strength training can be introduced at a very early training age, using the player's own body weight, together with medicine and Swiss ball exercises. These seem to work best for young players, especially if they are made fun.

Bouncing medicine balls can also contribute to improvement in motor coordination. However, coaches should ensure all exercises are high quality. Swiss ball exercises also contribute to core stabilisation and upper and lower body strength development, in addition to developing balance. All of these factors are essential in sport, but are especially important in tennis, when the player is often at the extremes of balance (eg the serve).

Musculoskeletal evaluation should begin at a very early training age. Ankle, knee, hip, trunk, spine and shoulder alignment, muscle imbalances and lack of flexibility should be evaluated regularly. Tennis is a one-sided sport in two dimensions (one arm only and different uses of anterior and posterior muscle groups) and imbalances need to be detected very early in young players.

Speed

The two windows of trainability for speed are:

- females aged 6–8 and 11–13

- males aged 7–9 and 13–16 (Viru et al 1998).

Peak speed velocity (PSpV) includes linear, lateral and multidirectional speed, agility and segmental speed. As discussed in Chapter 3, the first window for speed training of both females and males is not an energy system development, but central nervous system (CNS) training. It is important the CNS should be challenged with low volume and short-duration speed training. At this stage, anaerobic alactic power (see Glossary) is not available and interval training is not appropriate. This should only begin during the second window of accelerated adaptation to speed training (see Training to Train stage below).

Speed should be trained at every coaching session. Towards the end of the warm-up, or immediately after it, the player does not have any CNS or metabolic fatigue, so this is an optimal time to train speed. The training volume should be low and full recovery between exercises and sets is essential. Tennis requires acceleration over short distances (the maximum on a full court is around 12m), with proper posture and elbow and knee drive in the running action. Therefore, the development of quality movement is important.

Speed training, as well as segmental speed training, should take place regularly all-year-round and for all ages, irrespective of windows of trainability.

Skill

The development of physical literacy is of primary importance at this stage. Physical literacy is defined as the mastery of fundamental movement skills together with fundamental sports skills, and the ability to read the sporting environment (decision making).

The introduction of these activities is crucially important for future athletic development. These basic fundamental motor skills should be developed during this stage.

Specific tennis skills, including technical, tactical and mental/emotional skills, will be listed in the different stages of this case study. The coach needs to integrate these skills during coaching sessions. *The Space Between 6 and 16* poster, developed by the Lawn Tennis Association in 2002, lists the specific skills trainable at each age. It also recommends the type of competition, number of competitive matches per year and planning activities for each age and stage. Since 2002, detail behind the information on the *Space Between* poster has been developed.

In tennis, physical skills contribute to the technical skills, and mental and emotional skill levels are the principle determinant of tactical ability.

Recommendations for tennis-specific training at the FUNdamentals stage are listed below:

- Technical:

  – The basic shapes of ground strokes, serve and return should be a priority.

- Tactical:

  – The game situations of serving, returning and playing at the baseline.

  – Accuracy and consistency when playing.

- Type of competition:

  – Fun, playing in teams, local events or mini tennis leagues.

  – Modified scoring: best of three tiebreaks and short sets to fit with age.

- Number of tournament matches per year:

  – There should be a maximum of 20 formal individual matches, but any number of practice games, at the age of 8–9.

- Planning (weekly):

  – Six hours of physical activity, including tennis at 6–7 years of age.

  – Nine hours of physical activity at 9 years of age. Playing other sports is also very important.

  – Structured programmes of 2–4 tennis sessions a week at 8 years of age.

Players should also be introduced to the simple rules and ethics of sports at this stage.

Suppleness

The basics of flexibility training should be introduced through fun activities. Flexibility is a key training and performance factor in tennis. Optimal individual and sport-specific flexibility should be established at a very early training age. The window of optimal trainability for flexibility is 6–10 years of age.

Flexibility training should take place five to six times per week, if flexibility requires improvement. Two to three sessions of flexibility training each week, or flexibility training every other day, will maintain current levels. Stretching should not be done on rest days.

Structure/Stature

Chapter 2 explained the steady growth that characterises this stage. The average growth during the FUNdamental stage is approximately 5cm per year. Body alignment, flexibility and muscle imbalances should be evaluated regularly. Standing height, sitting height, arm span and weight should be measured on each birthday. In addition, quarterly standing height measurements are important. This process is described in Chapter 6.

(P)sychology

At the FUNdamentals stage, the mental skills of young players are quite specific. The aim for coaches should be to recognise the impact of their own coaching style in developing confidence and commitment. Positive coaching methods are essential for young players. Concentrating for long periods is difficult for players at this stage. Therefore, a variety of short-duration activities is recommended. Simple decision making is possible, but complex decision making is difficult. In tennis, coaches who spend time developing simple decision making with easy, tactical practices, will make player learning more fun. Mental skills training at this stage should be informal and depend on the positive learning environment created by the coach. Mental skills should be mixed into physical, technical and tactical training, so players develop them, without necessarily knowing they are doing so.

At this stage, tennis training focuses on:

- learning how to score and accept the score – tennis is an individual sport with an unusual scoring system and an undetermined time frame for matchplay
- learning how to win and lose
- respecting other players and coaches.

Sustenance

- **Nutrition and Hydration**

The role of the parents is obvious in providing optimum nutrition to the growing child. Parental education should develop the understanding that nutritional needs of a growing player cannot be based on scaled down adult recommendations (see football case study).

- Children tend to drink only when they are thirsty, which is too late, since they are already dehydrated. Coaches, therefore, need to include breaks in their sessions and educate young players on the importance of fluid intake.
- Hydration should be closely monitored through the first three stages of LTPD, especially before, during and after training and in hot weather. This is a critical variable to teach young children. Pre-pubescent children are inefficient at losing excess heat and can dehydrate and overheat very quickly. Young players at the FUNdamentals stage are less inhibited than they are at puberty, so if they are taught to check their urine output and colour, and are reminded about both, they quickly become proficient hydrators.

The above guidelines should be observed throughout the FUNdamentals, Learning to Play and Practice and Training to Train stages.

- **Rest**

Sleep is an important factor in rest. The recommendation for this age group is 8–10 hours of sleep per 24 hours.

The body is continually in the process of revitalisation, which peaks during what is known as Stage 3 and Stage 4 sleep. This is when the body increases secretion of the growth hormone (Coren, 1996).

Keeping a regular sleep schedule and creating an optimal sleeping environment is essential for young players.

- **Recovery – regeneration**

The coach is challenged to maximise adaptation by balancing training loads with appropriate recovery strategies, to suit the individual player. When players are young, strategies will have to be adapted so they are both understandable and relevant.

Young players need to be taught about:

- warm-up
- cool-down
- nutrition
- hydration.

They can also be introduced to simple ways of monitoring how they are feeling.

Smiley faces (Figure 26) have been used by a number of sports at all developmental stages. The young players must decide between three different faces (this range is in relation to their level of decision making).

The example below shows how young players can judge their level of fun. The coach could monitor tiredness or another factor by the same means. One of the most important variables to monitor at the FUNdamentals stage is **happiness**. At each training session, the child is asked to tick a box, or point to the face that best fits how they feel. With older players, the range of questions (variables) can be increased to include perceptions of fatigue, life at school, life at home, etc.

	☺	😐	☹
Fun			

Figure 26: Smiley faces

Schooling

School, tennis and other sport activities should be coordinated. School is an important part of young players' lives. Cognitive learning via school-based work is, of course, the priority. However, for a balanced, healthy and individual lifestyle, all aspects of development are equally important. Each of them can be easily complemented by physical activity.

Sociocultural

Coaches should recognise three important issues in the sociocultural development of young players:

- **lifestyle** – Young players need to be taught good hygiene, as well as the importance of good eating and sleeping habits during this stage. For coaches, this is part of developing the whole person.

- **socialisation via sport** – A number of important values and norms of society, such as looking after and thanking others, can be taught as young people take part in sport. These values and norms can, and should, be established at an early age.

- **sport socialisation** – Tennis has specific values and norms, such as rules, fairness, respect for the opponent and the game, and keeping score. These should all be taught from an early age.

Stage 2 – Learning to Play and Practice

This is the major motor learning stage for developing players (females aged 8–11 and males 9–12), with the most important period of motor development between the ages of 9–12 (Borms, 1986, Rushall, 1998 and Viru, 1995). During this time, children are developmentally ready to acquire the fundamental movement and sports skills considered the cornerstones of all athletic development.

The Philosophy of Coaching Tennis at the Learning to Play and Practice Stage

The fundamental skills of physical literacy should be taken to a higher level at this stage. In addition, the basic tennis technical skills should be put in place and mastered. Participation in other sports is still encouraged and considered important. From the beginning of this stage, young players are starting to play and compete on an individual basis, and are also ready to learn how to play doubles. They are maturing as people and beginning to understand the difference between effort and ability. They can recognise when another player is better, or not as good as they are. Young players compete to win, but winning and losing is still difficult for them to handle. Coaches and parents need to be clear about the importance of learning, developing and mastering skills for long-term development, and not be concerned with outcomes at this stage. For girls, many will be moving into puberty towards the end of the stage. The impact of early and late maturation will be important. Tactical development will increase in line with improved decision making. The role of the coach at this stage is paramount in progressing young players from the small court to the full court. Linked to this is the use of formal and adult scoring systems and, for the player with potential, the need to compete further away from home on occasions. However, training, rather than competition, remains the priority. The players will increase training volume towards the end of the stage. Tennis should still be fun and the source of friendships, although this can be more difficult in an individual sport. Increasing self-reliance is important.

The basics of the following ancillary capacities need to be taught at this stage, so they can be developed further in the later stages of athlete development:

- warm-up and cool-down
- stretching
- hydration and nutrition
- recovery and regeneration
- mental preparation
- simple tapering and peaking by the end of the stage
- pre-competition and in-competition routines
- post-competition recovery.

Periodisation

Up to the age of 9–10, young players should still have a structured and planned programme with unlimited and fun competition on a local and team basis. Appropriate equipment, courts and scoring systems are essential, so young players can progress appropriately.

However, after 10–11 for girls and 11–12 for boys, many talented young players are able and ready to play on a full-size court, with formal scoring and individual competition. The challenge for coaches with these players is to develop a periodised plan that will link sufficient and quality training for the age and stage, with the right level and volume of competition. Tennis is a sport in which young players could compete every weekend in term time and then every week in the school holidays, if they wanted to. Thus, ensuring sufficient and quality training time and appropriate competition is a major task for coaches. Many coaches have realised that discussing the principles of long-term development with parents, and involving them in the development process, has enabled effective planning of programmes that fit the real needs of each player at this age and stage.

Therefore, for a 10–11-year-old girl or a 11–12-year-old boy, a double periodised plan (two macrocycles) with two main periods of competition (in the spring and summer school holidays) and two extended periods of training in school term time, that also includes high quality training matches for a maximum of two weekend tournaments per month, in term time, is most appropriate.

The focus on training rather than competition is reflected in the more limited, but appropriate, competition schedule for this age of tennis player. Too many competitions decrease the amount of valuable training time and often do not help essential skill development for reaching potential. Conversely, not enough competition inhibits the development of competitive, mental, physical and tactical skills. For the development of the player, balance is critical.

The periodised plan (Figure 27) was designed for junior tennis players identified as having potential and who are at the end of the Learning to Play and Practice stage. Competitive phases in the spring and summer school holidays include domestic and international tournaments. Weekend training tournaments, played once or twice a month (maximum two matches per weekend) in term time, are domestic events. Family holidays, and rest and recovery periods, are included in the periodised plan (for other players, the schedule would be similar, but probably not include training matches in term time or as many tournaments in the summer holiday). **In tennis, the planning year starts in October and the competition year begins 1 January (week 1).**

The periodised annual plan for 10–11-year-old girls and 11–12-year-old boys with potential in the Learning to Play and Train stage has:

- Macrocycle 1 is 21 + 2 +2 + 2 + 3 + 1 microcycles (weeks)
- Macrocycle 2 is 9 + 1 + 2 + 6 + 3 microcycles (weeks).

The periodised year begins in October and the macrocycle consists of:

- 21 microcycles – 17 weeks of preparation, 4 weeks of recovery (October to December and January to March)
- 2 weeks of other sports (December)
- 2 microcycles of specific preparation (March)
- 2 microcycles of pre-competition (March)
- 3 microcycles of competition (April)
- 1 week of rest (late April).

The second macrocycle consists of:

- 9 microcycles – 7 weeks of preparation, 2 weeks of recovery (May to June)
- 1 microcycle of specific preparation (July)
- 2 microcycles of pre-competition (July)
- 6 microcycles of competition (July and August)
- 3 weeks of rest and recovery (September).

A microcycle lasts for seven days.

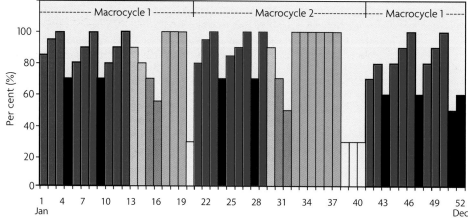

Figure 27: Annual periodised plan for a 10–11-year-old girl or a 11–12-year-old boy in the Learning to Play and Practice stage training load (volume + intensity)

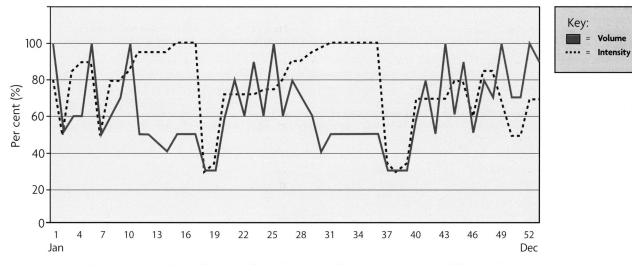

Figure 28: Annual periodised plan for a 10–11-year-old girl or a 11–12-year-old boy in the Learning to Play and Practice stage (volume and intensity)

Training to Competition Ratios

In generic terms, an 80:20 training to competition ratio is recommended by experts for the Learning to Play and Practice stage. However, this varies according to the sport and specific individual needs. For tennis players up to the age of 9–10, the ratio is satisfactory. For those aged 10–11, who have a periodised plan, the training to competition ratio is 65:35. This gives young players the opportunity to prepare, in addition to becoming a well-trained competitor in both the short and long term.

The 10 Ss of Training and Performance During the Learning to Play and Practice Stage

Since this is the major skill learning stage, motor skill development should be emphasised.

Stamina, strength, speed and suppleness should be further improved by well-sequenced and integrated training. Although there is less interference between training adaptations of different factors during the FUNdamental and Learning to Play and Practice stages, a well-structured and periodised training, competition and recovery programme, such as that shown above, should further optimise training.

Stamina

At this stage, endurance should be maintained through fun activities. Very short interval training for improvement could be used if needed.

Strength

Short-term strength training at this stage does not seem to interfere with endurance training. However, unlike adults, the maintenance of strength gains with this age group cannot be achieved with one session per microcycle. Strength training should be done at least twice a week, but should not exceed 30 minutes per session.

Speed

Speed training should be undertaken at every training session in a similar way to the FUNdamental stage. It is recommended this should be towards the end of the warm-up, or immediately after it, before players are tired. Training volume should be low and there should be full recovery between exercises and sets. Tennis requires acceleration over short distances (the maximum is about 15m). Players should maintain proper posture, with elbow and knee drive in the running action. They also need to move quickly, both laterally and diagonally. Coaches should spend time working on this aspect of speed training.

Speed training and segmental speed training should take place regularly, throughout the year, and for all ages, irrespective of the windows of trainability or the phase of the annual plan.

Skill

It is essential coaches develop fundamental movement skills and sports skills between the ages of 8–11 in girls and 9–12 in boys. If these skills are not developed before puberty, they may not be fully trained at a later time, although carefully planned and early remedial programmes can contribute to limited success.

For the Learning to Play and Practice stage, the recommendations for tennis-specific training are:

- Technical:

  – All the basic strokes should be well developed, with increasing racket head speed.

- Tactical:

  – All game situations of serving, receiving the serve, playing on the baseline, approaching or playing at the net, and playing against an opponent who is approaching or at the net, should be taught.

  – Doubles should be included in the programme.

- Type of competition:

  – Full court and full set scoring towards the end of the stage.

  – Club, league, county, national and international towards the end of the stage.

- Number of tournament matches per year:

  – There should be a maximum of 40 individual matches, with unlimited practice matches, at age 11.

- Planning (annual):

  – Two periods of training with two periods of competition (double periodisation, two macrocycles).

  – Twelve hours of physical activity in a training week at age 11, with other sports still being important.

  – Five hours of tennis-specific training per training week.

Suppleness

This stage is a sensitive window of trainability to improve flexibility. Flexibility training should take place five to six times per week, if improvement is required. Two to three sessions of flexibility training each week, or every other day, will maintain current flexibility levels. Stretching should not be done on rest days.

Structure/Stature

This stage is characterised by a period of steady growth. The average growth during this stage is 5–6cm per year (see Chapter 4).

Measuring standing height, sitting height and arm span at least once a year is important. Once the onset of PHV is identified, measurements of standing height should be increased to every three months (quarterly) or more frequently. Some early maturers will start their growth spurt towards the end of this phase, so monitoring the onset of PHV is crucial.

(P)sychology

The importance of coaching behaviour is paramount in order for players to feel confident and able to learn from their mistakes, as well as their successes. At this stage, players can be introduced to structured mental training, and their mental and emotional development gives the opportunity for a number of new skills to be learnt. The aim is to introduce players to the following relevant skills for this stage and for tennis:

- commitment

- self-confidence

- concentration

- self-reliance

- working with others

- motivation.

As in the FUNdamentals stage, coaches should attempt to keep mental skills training realistic and fun. In addition, this training should be a normal part of practice, as it is just as important as physical and technical practice. The atmosphere in the coaching environment should reinforce the mental skills being taught. Competition can be stressful for a young player and coaches should ensure the player is supported and able to learn, whatever the outcome. Winning is important, but at this stage, the process of learning is equally important.

Sustenance

• Nutrition and Hydration

The guidelines outlined in the FUNdamentals stage should be reinforced. Parents are very important in providing optimum nutrition for the child. As players grow older, they become more responsible and learn when and what to eat before, during and after matches and training. They also become old enough to know when to drink adequately, and how to recognise the early signs of dehydration. Reminders about hydration will be easy to reinforce if the player has developed a habit of checking urine volume and colour during the FUNdamentals stage.

• Rest

The recommendation for this age group is 8–10 hours of sleep per 24 hours. Young players at this stage need adequate levels of sleep, especially as training and competitive volumes are gradually increased and/or the onset of PHV is noted.

• Recovery – regeneration

In principle, players need to be taught two things:

1. To monitor their recovery by identifying specific fatigue and the type of recovery they need.

2. To manage their recovery by looking after themselves properly.

These two concepts apply to every player at all stages of development and sporting experience, because they are linked closely to long-term training adaptations. They are, however, sometimes difficult concepts for young players to grasp. For coaches, monitoring performance and fatigue in players provides a measure of the effectiveness of training. In addition, consistent and systematic monitoring can pre-empt potential adaptation problems. It enables the coach to identify specific recovery strategies relevant to the individual player's maturation level, training stress and lifestyle.

The range of variables that can be monitored increases as the player's cognitive skills improve and with the onset of PHV. At the FUNdamentals stage, it was suggested players rate themselves in the form of smiley faces. At the Learning to Play and Practice stage, players could use a set of numbers from 1–3 or 1–5, as a quick gauge of their feelings of adaptation and wellness.

The main variables to be monitored at this stage include:

- fatigue
- self-esteem
- quality of sleep
- illness or injuries.

Schooling

At this stage, the same issues that were important in FUNdamentals should continue to be applied. However, towards the end of this stage, players are moving into secondary education. For many young people, moving to the generally larger and more impersonal secondary school can be a daunting experience and one that can impact on confidence, even in tennis. Any conflict with school sports, other school activities and tennis should be avoided.

Sociocultural

In addition to developing different lifestyle management skills with changes in schooling and beginning to play as an individual in competition, young players need to improve and develop social skills through sport. More and different competition will highlight the importance of knowing and understanding the social requirements of the sport. The coach should be concerned with developing all these skills, as well as building the support team around the player.

Stage 3 – Training to Train

This stage forms the foundation of aerobic and strength fitness for female players (11–15 years) and of aerobic fitness for males (12–16 years). Both genders should develop further speed capacities, taking advantage of the second speed window of trainability in speed training. Players are able to internalise the advanced techniques in physical, technical and recovery training, and improve their knowledge base of ancillary capacities as they mature. Although this knowledge base was introduced at the Learning to Play and Practice stage, coaching can be expanded as a result of increased understanding.

The majority of players will reach puberty during this stage. The onset of PHV should be used as a reference point to design programmes for the pubertal player on an individual basis.

Periodisation

In tennis, double periodisation can be successful until the age of 12. From 13–14, triple periodisation (three macrocycles in a year) can be an optimal framework of preparation, competition and recovery (with a move to multiple periodisation after 16). Figures 29 and 30 illustrate a triple periodised annual plan for a 15-year-old girl. The plan is linked to regional, national, domestic and international tournament schedules, depending on the success of the player. There are three main competitive phases in school holiday periods, but the player is also likely to play a two-match tournament over at least one weekend per month, during term time.

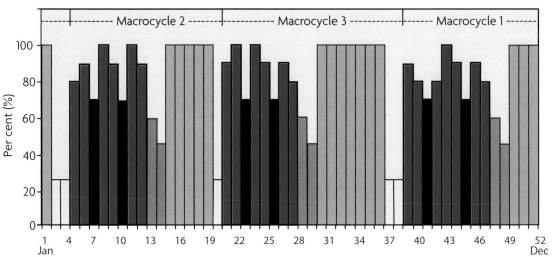

Figure 29: Annual triple periodised plan for a 15-year-old girl at the Training to Train stage

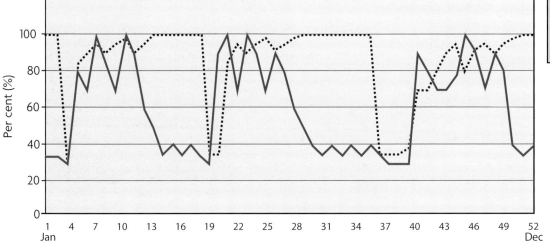

Figure 30: Annual periodised plan for a 15-year-old girl at the Training to Train stage training load (volume and intensity)

Note: These are sample plans which should be adjusted to suit the individual needs of the player.

The triple periodised annual plan (Figures 29 and 30) begins in October:

The first macrocycle is 17 weeks in length from October to January and has:

- 9 microcycles – 7 weeks of preparation, 2 weeks of recovery (October and November)
- 2 microcycles – pre-competition (November and December)
- 4 microcycles – competition (December and January)
- 2 week – rest.

The second macrocycle is 16 weeks in length from January to April and has:

- 8 microcycles – 6 weeks of preparation, 2 weeks of recovery (January to March)
- 2 microcycles – pre-competition (March)
- 5 microcycles – competition (March and April)
- 1 week – rest.

The third macrocycle is 19 weeks in length from May to September and has:

- 8 microcycles – 6 weeks of preparation, 2 weeks of recovery (May and June)
- 2 microcycles – pre-competition (July)
- 7 microcycles – competition (July and August)
- 2 weeks – rest (September).

Training to Competition Ratios

In general terms, the training to competition ratio (including competition-specific training) of 60:40 is recommended for the Training to Train stage. This ratio varies a little in tennis, according to individual needs. Again, players undertaking this ratio of training to competition will be better prepared for competition in both the short and long term, than those who focus solely on competing and winning.

The 10 Ss of Training and Performance During the Training to Train Stage

Stamina

The onset of PHV contributes to accelerated adaptation in the aerobic system. This acceleration is known as peak aerobic velocity (see Chapter 3).

During training, females aged 11–15 and males aged 12–16 should be grouped according to biological maturation, rather than chronological age. As described in the case study in Chapter 4, early and late maturation in young adolescents may be four to five years apart.

Training should be organised so early, average and late maturers are in different training groups, or have their own training programme that matches their developmental age and particular needs. This allows training to be based upon maturation levels and not chronological age. This is important to reduce the likelihood of under or overtraining occurring, if all players train together. If players are all trained together at this stage, only a small percentage of each chronological age group will be properly trained and the critical period of accelerated adaptation of the aerobic system may be compromised.

Early, average or late maturers should then be regrouped regularly after training with their peer group. Removing young players from their peer group may result in negative, mental and emotional outcomes.

Non-weight-bearing aerobic activities at this stage help prevent injuries, such as Osgood Schlatter's. If players sustain pain associated with growth, a reduction in technical-tactical training and weight-bearing activities should be considered. Most of the aerobic training for this age group should be in the form of non-weight-bearing activity. In addition, very short interval training can be used as a weight-bearing activity, with the bonus that this develops the aerobic system in parallel with the anaerobic system.

Strength

The onset of PHV will determine the extent and frequency of weight training during the Training to Train stage. The critical periods of accelerated adaptation to strength training will occur towards the end of, and immediately after, PHV for females, and 12–18 months after PHV for males (see Chapter 3).

With the onset of PHV, proper Olympic lifting techniques should be introduced to players by appropriately trained experts (eg a UK strength and conditioning accredited coach). At this time, there is an accelerated period of adaptation to strength training (peak strength velocity or PSV). Players should master basic lifting techniques as an injury prevention measure, and to enhance optimal adaptation to strength training.

The increase in body mass (peak weight velocity or PWV) will occur after PHV. The ideal scenario for the coach is to start free-weight training earlier with those players who experience the early onset of PWV, and later for those with a late PWV onset.

Coaches should monitor their players for the onset of PHV and PHV itself. These measurements accurately indicate the proper time to implement free-weight programmes.

Speed

The second window for accelerated speed adaptation is 11–13 years of age for females and 13–16 for males (see Chapter 3). Although CNS training is important, anaerobic alactic power (up to 5 seconds) and anaerobic alactic capacity (between 5 and 20 seconds) interval training should be introduced at the Training to Train stage. For females, this should be during the first part of the stage and for males, during the latter part. Progressive overloading is essential for adaptation to take place. Linear, lateral and multidirectional movement speed should be trained by proper sequencing of speed work with other training activities. Lateral and multidirectional speed are important aspects of tennis.

As outlined in both the FUNdamentals and Learning to Play and Practice stages, speed should be trained all-year-round, regardless of the different phases and objectives of the annual plan. This training should take place at the end of the warm-up, when there is no metabolic or nervous system fatigue present. The volume of training should be low.

Speed training should be in the form of anaerobic alactic power or CNS work and anaerobic alactic capacity work. Since there is no accumulated metabolic or CNS fatigue at the end of speed work, there is no interference with other short- or long-term objectives of training.

Skill

Players experience rapid growth during adolescence. This growth includes changes in leg, trunk and arm length, with a resultant change in the centre of gravity. However, the body does not grow in proportion: different parts of the body grow at different rates and times in different players. As a result, movement skills and technical skills should be carefully monitored during PHV, because players may experience temporary difficulties (poor coordination and clumsiness) in skill execution. Coaches should be patient with these players during and immediately after PHV and explain to them what is happening as they mature.

Recommendations for tennis-specific training at the Training to Train stage are as follows:

- Technical:
  - Developing power and the use of spin on ground strokes and serve.
  - Developing additional stokes.
- Tactical:
  - Playing offensively.
  - Playing with an individual games style.
  - Using specific tactics on different surfaces.
- Type of competition:
  - Club, league, county, national and international.
- Number of tournament matches per year:
  - There should be a maximum of 70 individual matches, but unlimited training matches, at age 14.
- Planning (annual):
  - Triple periodisation (three macrocycles in a year) of training, competition and recovery.
  - At age 14, there should be 24 hours of physical activity in a training week, including other sports.
  - At least 12 hours of tennis-specific training per week.

Suppleness

Flexibility should be monitored carefully in the Training to Train stage. Static stretching and proprioceptive neuromuscular facilitation (PNF) should be complemented by active isolated stretching when required. A stretching session should be separate from other training activities and is recommended during this, and the next, stage of player development. In principle, static stretching and PNF should be performed two hours prior to, or two hours after, training and/or competition activities.

Structure/Stature

The Training to Train stage addresses critical periods of physical skill development (endurance, strength, speed and flexibility) and technical skill development. This is the most complex stage in LTAD. Players who fail to exploit the windows of trainability during this stage may never reach their full potential, regardless of subsequent remedial programmes. A major reason why so many players plateau during the later stage of their careers is primarily due to an overemphasis on competition, rather than training, during this important period in their athletic development.

Viru (1995) and Viru et al (1998) stated: 'If there is conflict between the long-term plan and the competition demands, the first must take priority.'

Increases in stature are characterised by rapid acceleration of growth after the onset of PHV and rapid deceleration of growth after PHV. Measurements of standing height, sitting height and arm span should be taken every three months (or more frequently), to monitor those body segments that are growing fastest.

During this stage, the aerobic window should be identified by the onset of PHV, and the second speed window by chronological age. Coaches need to be aware of early, average and late maturers.

According to Tanner (1989), a male typically grows about 7cm in the first year after the onset of PHV, 9cm in the second and 7cm in the third. This is followed by 3cm of growth in the year after PHV and about 2cm thereafter, until secession of growth around 18–20 years of age.

The increase in height for girls is less, with measurements of 6cm, 8cm and 6cm during the three years of PHV. This increase in height for girls will also typically occur two years before boys.

During PHV:

- the shoulders widen in boys
- the hips widen more in girls
- muscles increase in size and strength more in boys than girls
- as a rule, leg length reaches its peak length and is 6–9 months ahead of maximum trunk length
- shoulder and chest width are the last segments to reach peak growth.

Peak muscle growth velocity occurs 6–12 months after PHV.

The implications of this are important and impact training in a sport like tennis. They determine differences in technical skills and, thus, tactical abilities between boys and girls. The way in which men and women play the game is different because of the physical differences in structure and stature.

A rapid or slow transit through PHV can have an effect on players. Transit refers to the length of time an individual takes to move through the growth spurt. A rapid transit for a player would be 1.5 years, but another individual could experience slow transit and take 4–5 years, or more, to reach full maturity.

Rapid transit can have a detrimental impact on skill levels, and on speed, strength, power and flexibility adaptation. Coaches should advise players and parents on the consequences of rapid transit through puberty.

(P)sychology

The aim of this stage is to introduce players to more advanced mental skills training because their mental and emotional development warrants this, and the individual nature of the sport requires it. Building on the skills introduced in the FUNdamentals and Learning to Play and Practice stages, this stage in tennis will focus on advancing the variety of psychological skills learnt by the age group.

These are:

- concentration and focus
- self-discipline
- anxiety control
- goal setting
- self-reliance
- self-talk
- imagery
- routines (pre-competition, during points and between games)
- taking pride in, and responsibility for, performance.

Sustenance

• Nutrition and Hydration

The guidelines described in the FUNdamentals and Learning to Play and Practice stages should be applied at this stage. Nutritional supplements can be added to the guidelines during the growth spurt, especially with girls, as they begin menarche. Sports drinks should be used during and after training and competition as rehydration.

• Rest

The guidelines described in the previous two stages should be applied here. In addition, players of this age could try to sleep for a short time during the afternoon. This should be for about half an hour: doing so will enhance the functioning of the CNS for several hours, resulting in better decision making.

• Recovery – regeneration

This is a critical developmental stage that can have a lasting effect on the sporting potential and future health of the individual. During this stage, young players are exposed to increased training loads at the same time as they are experiencing rapid physical changes. Increased growth, especially of muscle, bone and connective tissue, together with hormonal changes, leads to an increase in mechanical loading requirements for the individual. From a coaching standpoint, all these factors require careful management.

The Training to Train stage is a very stressful time emotionally because most young players are studying hard for career-determining exams. They are also experiencing increased social and psychological challenges from their peers and family.

More than any other developmental stage, this is the one that can expose the gifted athlete to overtraining, overuse injuries and burnout. For these reasons, it is paramount the coach and player monitor individual adaptation by keeping a record of training loads, performances and the player's responses to these and other stresses.

Each player should have a personalised training diary in which to keep this data. Unfortunately, experience shows player compliance rates for recording information consistently and reliably is often poor. Players should record:

- resting heart rates (RHR)
- body weight
- quality of sleep
- fatigue levels.

While the reliability and usefulness of RHR can be debated, regular recording of these variables trains players to be more perceptive about their adaptation to training and to their general well-being. Parents could be recruited to help young players develop the habit of keeping a training diary. Coaches should ensure they take regular interest in the information.

In addition to the five variables listed on page 70, the daily checklist should also include ratings for:

- self-esteem

- muscle soreness

- appetite

- external stresses (at home and school)

- illness or injury

- menstrual cycle and any issues for girls.

If a female has not started menstruation by the time she is 16, she faces increased future health risks, so it is important she consults a suitably qualified medical specialist for advice.

This is a critical stage for developing players to be introduced to medical and sports science screening and regular testing. In particular, musculoskeletal evaluations are critical to identify any of the common growth problems (especially, in tennis, those of the spine, shoulders, hips and lower limbs) associated with PHV.

Tennis is a one-sided sport and also has inconsistencies in muscle strength between the front and back of the upper body. Regular testing and monitoring is essential, especially of the spine and shoulder, to ensure young players are developing well and are not incurring the likelihood of future injury.

Schooling

At this stage, many young players are studying for exams. Overstress should be monitored carefully during PHV. Overstress refers to an excess of the normal every day stresses that can impact on the player. These include school issues and exams, peer groups, family, relationships and increasing training volume and intensities. A good balance should be established between these factors, with the coach, player and parents working together. Conflict between school sports, other school activities and tennis training and competition should be avoided.

Sociocultural

During the Training to Train stage, young players will often be travelling to training and tournaments, both domestically and internationally. The sporting experience should be taken beyond the tennis courts and hotel rooms. If cultural activities are well-organised and integrated, they should not interfere with or distract from training or competition. Such activities help young players experience events and places outside tennis for short periods of time, and players will be relaxed and ready to practise and compete when they return. Opportunities to experience different countries and cultures, geography, history, architecture, literature, music, cuisine and national sports should form part of the education of young players. Sadly, many coaches (and parents) are so pre-occupied with training and competition that they neglect the wonderful opportunities to enhance their young players' experiences.

Conclusion

The challenge for coaches in any sport is to manage the complexities of growth and maturation in the development of young people, while ensuring all training and performance factors are considered. In these two case studies, the factors that affect different stages of development have been grouped together as the 10 Ss of training and performance.

Throughout this resource, attention has been drawn to the facts of growth and maturation, and the use of sensitive periods of trainability and biological markers in the development of young players.

Coaches will probably already be familiar with the stages of LTAD. These case studies have examined in detail the first three stages of:

- FUNdamentals

- Learning to Play and Practice

- Training to Train.

These three stages are impacted to the greatest extent by the process of the growth and maturation process that takes place in every young person.

The demands of players and the sports of football and tennis have been examined and discussed. Both have identified the critical periods of trainability for each stage and presented sport-specific information for coaches. In this way, it is possible for the needs of each player in the different stages to be met, in order to maximise potential and ensure coaches understand the skills and requirements for each player at each stage. There are many similarities between the studies, despite the fact football and tennis are very different sports. The similarities arise from the fact that both sports are working with the same age groups of players as they move through their careers. Young players are people first and sportspeople second. Reference has been made to structured programmes and periodisation as planning tools, which coaches should use to integrate and sequence the 10 Ss at each stage. The importance of developing the key factors of the 10 Ss at different stages cannot be overestimated, because they link closely to the critical periods of trainability and the biological markers for young players. With careful integration of all these factors, coaches in both sports should be able to develop young players to their potential.

References

Bangsbo, J. (1994) 'The physiology of soccer, with special reference to intense intermittent exercise,' *Acta Physiologica Scandinavica Supplement*, 619: 1–155.

Bangsbo, J., Iaia, F.M. and Krustrup, P. (2007) 'Metabolic response and fatigue in soccer,' *International Journal of Sports Physiology and Performance*, 2: 111–127.

Bangsbo, J., Mohr, M. and Krustrup, P. (2006) 'Physical and metabolic demands of training and matchplay in the elite football player,' *Journal of Sports Science*, 24(7): 665–674.

Bar-Or, O. (1996) 'Developing the pre-pubertal athlete; physiological principles', in Hollander, A.P., Strasse, D., Cappaert, J.M. and Trappe, T.A. (eds) (1996) *Biomechanics and Medicine in Swimming VII*. London: E & FN Spon. ISBN: 978-0-419204-80-0: 135–139.

Bar-Or, O. (2000) 'Nutritional considerations for the child athlete', *Canadian Journal of Applied Physiology*. 26 (Suppl.):186–191.

Borms, J. (1986) 'The Child and exercise: an overview,' *Journal of Sport Sciences*, 4: 3–20.

Calder, A. (2003) 'Recovery' (Ch. 14) in Reid, M., Quinn, A. and Crespo, M. (eds) (2003) *Strength and Conditioning for Tennis*. Roehampton: International Tennis Federation. ISBN: 1-903013-19-4.

Coren, S. (1996) *Sleep Thieves*. London: Simon & Schuster Ltd. ISBN: 978-0-684823-04-1.

Lawn Tennis Association (2002) *The Space Between 6 and 16*. Poster.

Paish, W. (1991) *Training for peak performance*. London: A & C Black. ISBN: 978-0-713634-04-4.

Rienzi, E., Drust, B., Reilly, T., Carter, J.E.L. and Martin, A. (2000) 'Investigation of anthropometric and work-rate profiles of elite South American international soccer players,' *Journal of Sports Medicine and Physical Fitness*, 40: 162–169.

The Football Association (2006) *Introductory Guide to Women's and Girls' Football*.

Reid, M., Quinn, A., and Crespo, M. (2003) *Strength and Conditioning for Tennis*. Roehampton: International Tennis Federation. ISBN: 1-903013-19-4.

Rushall, B. (1998) 'The growth of physical characteristics in male and female children', in *Sports Coach*, Vol.20, Summer: 25–27.

Tanner, J.M. (1989) *Foetus into Man: Physical Growth from Conception to Maturity*. Hertfordshire. Castlemead Publications. ISBN: 978-0-948555-24-4.

Viru, A. (1995) *Adaptation in Sports Training*. CRC Press: Boca Raton. ISBN: 978-0-849301-71-1.

Viru, A, Loko, J., Volver, A., Laaneots, L., Karlesom, K. and Viru, M. (1998) 'Age periods of accelerated improvements of muscle strength, power, speed and endurance in age interval 6–18 years', in *Biology of Sport*, 15 (4): 211–227.

Further Reading

Bunker, D., Thorpe, R. and Almond, L. (1986) *Rethinking Games Teaching*. Loughborough: Loughborough University.

Dick, F. (2007) *Sports Training Principles*. London: A & C Black Publishers Ltd. ISBN: 978-0-713682-78-6.

Morris, J.G and Nevill, M.E. (2007) *A sporting chance – enhancing opportunities for high-level sporting performance: influence of relative age*. Loughborough University.

Pankhurst, A. (2007) *Planning and Periodisation*. Leeds: Coachwise Business Solutions/The National Coaching Foundation. ISBN: 978-1-905540-43-3.

Stafford, I. (2005) *Coaching for Long-term Athlete Development: to improve participation and performance in sport*. Leeds: Coachwise Business Solutions/The National Coaching Foundation. ISBN: 978-1-902523-70-5.

LIVERPOOL JOHN MOORES UNIVERSITY LEARNING SERVICES

Chapter 6: Tracking Growth and Development – How to Measure PHV

Introduction

Throughout this resource, the importance of PHV as a measure of growth and maturation has been emphasised. Coaches will understand the significance of PHV:

- in planning programmes for young performers

- as a benchmark to plan for, and develop, the potential of young performers.

Chapter 2 highlighted some of the important factors that could be measured as indicators of growth and development. This chapter concentrates specifically on the measurement of stature as an indicator of PHV. It gives coaches information on how to:

1. measure stature accurately

2. plot growth rates by use of distance and velocity curves

3. calculate the age at PHV

4. estimate other indices of maturity

5. understand the strengths and weaknesses of each method.

This chapter includes the following sections:

1. Tools and equipment for measurement

2. Recording measurements

3. How to measure

4. When to measure

5. Why measurement accuracy is important

6. Other recommended measurements

7. Advanced measurement techniques

8. Ethical and sensitive issues

9. Implications for coaches

10. Conclusion.

1. Tools and Equipment for Measurement

High-quality training programmes require the consideration of a number of variables, all of which concern the performer. The maturation level, with stature as an indicator, is one variable for young developing performers. The accuracy level of the measurement of stature is important and depends on the use of appropriate and correct equipment, as well as standard measuring procedures. Inevitably, the more expensive the equipment, the more likely it is to give relevant and accurate information.

Equipment can be divided into at least three categories: ideal, acceptable and unacceptable.

Ideal equipment could include a permanent wall-mounted or free-standing stadiometer (see Figure 31). Such a stadiometer should have a sliding headboard and a dial or digital read out.

Acceptable equipment could include:

- an anthropometer or retractable steel measuring tape

- a headboard

- a measuring platform, about 1m$_2$, made of standard plywood (preferably with adjustable feet to ensure a level surface).

Unacceptable equipment and procedures include:

- the use of a cloth measuring tape

- a headboard made of flexible material, such as paper or cardboard

- a carpeted or uneven floor surface

- the lack of a back board.

Figure 31: A stadiometer

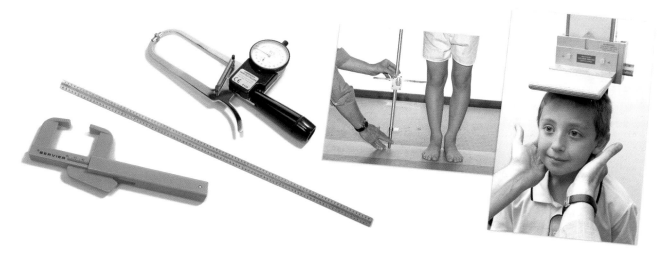

Figure 32: A range of equipment

2. Recording Measurements

As PHV is dependent on the accurate measurement of stature, measurements need to be made to the nearest 0.1cm.

The protocol for recording measurements is important and should be consistent.

- When measuring stature, two measurements should be recorded for each performer and these should not differ by more than 0.4cm. If this is achieved, the average of the two scores is calculated and recorded as the stature of the performer at that time.

- If measurements differ by more than 0.4cm, a third measurement is required, in order to calculate the median of the three measurements. The median score is calculated by ranking the three scores from lowest to highest, with the middle score as the median.

An example of recording and calculation is shown in examples 1 and 2.

Example 1	
Stature measurement 1	166.2cm
Stature measurement 2	166.4cm
The above two measurements are within the acceptable range, because they do not differ by more than 0.4cm. The average (mean) measurement recorded is 166.3cm.	

Example 2	
Stature measurement 1	158.2cm
Stature measurement 2	162.9cm
Stature measurement 3	162.6cm
In this example, the first two measurements differ by more than 0.4cm, so a third measurement is required. The median of the three scores has been calculated and recorded as 162.6cm.	

Coaching reflection point: In the above examples, what factors do you think might have caused a low score on the first stature measurement?

Key Concepts and Summary

Stature should be measured to the nearest 0.1cm or 1mm. Two measurements should be taken, but a third will be required if the two stature results differ by 0.4cm or 4mm. If two measurements were taken, the mean of the two results should be recorded. If three measurements were registered, the median would be recorded.

3. How to Measure

Although measuring stature may be considered a straightforward task, the techniques required need considerable attention to detail, if results are to be valid.

As examples 1 and 2 show, it is easy to have large variations in scores for the same performer.

The protocol for taking measurements is important, in order to reduce error.

Ideally, two measurers should be present: one to move the performer into the required position, while the second records the actual measurement. If a second measurer is not available, one measurer can conduct the measurement of stature. However, extra attention should be paid to the technique.

Recommended Protocol

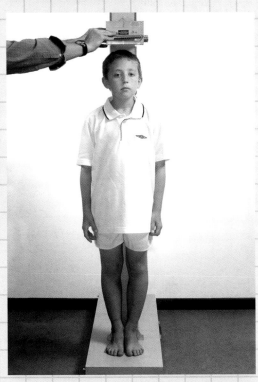

Figure 33: Performer standing on a stadiometer

Figure 34: Frankfort plane

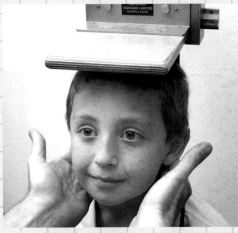

Figure 35: Gentle stretching of the neck

1. Two adults should undertake the measuring process. This task should not be undertaken in isolation with children and young people.

2. The process should be fully explained to the performer, including the reasons why it is necessary and what direct handling is required. Their verbal consent should be sought on each occasion they are measured. The measuring process and the frequency with which it will be undertaken should be explained to parents at the time the performer joins the programme and their written consent obtained.

3. The performer should be asked to remove shoes/trainers and socks before being positioned on a level surface. Heels, buttocks, the upper part of the back and back of the head should be against a vertical wall or door. The stadiometer should have sliding headboards and a dial or digital read out.

4. The performer should stand straight, with heels and toes together and arms relaxed and hanging by the side of the body.

5. The measurer should now position the performer's head in what is known as the Frankfort plane (Figure 34). This is an imaginary horizontal line running from the orbital (lower part of eye socket) to the tragion (the 'flappy' notch in the middle of the entrance to the ear). This should be done by placing both hands just behind the performer's ears (along the mastoid process – that is, the angle of the jaw), ensuring the eyes are looking directly ahead.

6. A slight upward stretch is then applied at the mastoid process. This is necessary because the body is prone to variations in stature throughout the day, due to compression of the discs in the spine. Therefore, people are slightly shorter at the end of the day compared to measurements taken in the morning. Care should be taken to avoid excessive upward stretching.

7. If stature measurements are taken against a wall, the headboard needs to be placed firmly on the highest point of the head, ensuring any hair is flattened. Performers wearing hairclips or bands will need to remove these, if considered obstructive.

8. The measurer instructs the performer to stand tall (ensuring the performer's heels are not lifted off the floor), take a deep breath, stretch up and lower shoulders. Height will be measured on the 'stretch up and lower shoulders' command.

9. Measurement should be of the greatest distance from the floor to the vertex (top) of the head.

10. The natural tendency for children and adolescents is to tense their bodies, thus lifting their shoulders, head and heels. Measurers need to be aware of this.

11. If a pencil mark (indicating the performer's stature) is to be made on the wall or on paper stuck on a wall, it should be level with the underside of the headboard. Alternatively, if using a stadiometer, this equipment has a counter dial which presents the score automatically for recording purposes.

12. Once the performer has moved away, the distance between the mark and the floor can be measured using a measuring tape (a metal retractable tape is recommended) to the nearest 0.1cm.

4. When to Measure

Stature should be recorded as and when necessary. The intervals between testing sessions need to be long enough for substantial growth to occur over and above the 0.4cm expected from measurement error.

Performers might become too preoccupied with their measurements, particularly if they perceive they are not growing as fast as their counterparts.

Finally, the performer can become bored if stature is recorded too frequently.

Key Concepts and Summary

Other considerations:

- It is recommended measurements be taken once every three months.

- Measurements should be taken as close as possible to the same date in the month and also at the same time of day.

- Since training sessions are often at the same time of day, it would be sensible to devote part of one training session to recording stature.

- If possible, stature measurements should be taken following a day of rest, to prevent confounding training effects from the previous day.

- Taking measurements at the start of training sessions would be ideal to prevent the performer being prone to any of its effects. For example, differences might occur between stretching or bounding drop-jump sessions, which can impact on stature.

The question of when to start measuring is dependent on a number of factors, such as:

- how long the coach is likely to train the performer

- the objective for using growth measurements for training

- how soon techniques and the environment for measuring growth can be achieved.

Peak Height Velocity

If the coach suspects the performer has reached PHV, measurements should be taken every three months in a 12-month period, to determine if this is the case. Since the range in which PHV typically occurs is between 10–12 years for girls and 13.5–14.5 years for boys (Freeman et al 1995 and Tanner et al 1966a and b), it would be beneficial to have as many measurement points as possible, prior to the onset of PHV (1–4 measurements per year). Once PHV has been determined, measurements should be continued until cessation of growth.

This period of development and maturation can make young people self-conscious about their bodies and vulnerable to the impact of any perceived negativity about their growth rate, body shape and weight, particularly in relation to their peers. Sensitivity needs to be shown and great care taken to ensure they are not made to feel uncomfortable or vulnerable as a result of the measurement process.

A distance and velocity graph can be created, even if the coach only has yearly measurements up to the time when he is considering measuring more frequently. The objective of the graph is to show the height of the performer on several occasions and is plotted against age, to indicate how much, and how rapidly, the performer has grown. If data is plotted on Child Growth Foundation national percentile charts (see Appendix 1), it is possible to determine at what percentile the performer's height is for their age, compared to the average for children in the UK[1].

Children tend to maintain their position on growth charts during childhood. However, during adolescence, this will often change because of individual differences in the timing and tempo of the growth spurt. As a result, growth charts must be interpreted carefully during adolescence.

Table 1 presents the stature of a football player plotted between the ages of 6–20. Measurements were performed only once a year around the performer's birthday.

Table 1: Annual stature measurements recorded for one male football player between the ages of 6–20

Age	6	7	8	9	10	11	12	13	14	15	16	17	18	19	20
Ht (cm)	124	124.5	129	133.2	139	145.3	150.1	156.7	167.2	170.5	172.8	175.9	177.2	179.1	184

The above data can be plotted as a graph to show height at any given time.

---

[1] All growth reference charts are intended to be descriptive of growth patterns and are, therefore, used as reference values and not prescriptive standards.

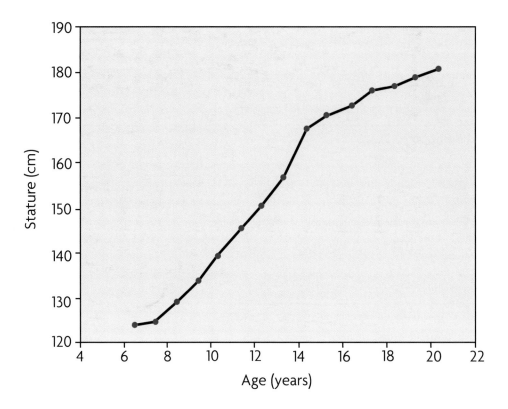

Figure 36: A distance curve for a male, recorded between the ages of 6–20, showing stature at different ages

The graph enables the velocity curve to be determined. As a result, PHV can be ascertained. To calculate this, the increase in stature must be subtracted from one measurement to the next consecutive measurement. For example, in Table 2 (below), the increase in stature from 9.3 years to 10.3 years is 5.8cm. The yearly change in centimetres against decimal age can also be plotted. (Coaches can use Appendix 3 at the end of this chapter for an explanation of decimal age and how it can be calculated.)

Table 2: The change in stature (cm) from one year to the next for a male performer

Age	6.45 – 7.44	7.44 – 8.399	8.399 – 9.389	9.389 – 10.362	10.362 – 11.406	11.406 – 12.362	12.362 – 13.321	13.321 – 14.389	14.389 – 15.291	15.291 – 16.45	16.45 – 17.406	17.406 – 18.399	18.399 – 19.422	19.422 – 20.422
Ht (cm)	0.5	4.5	4.2	5.8	6.3	4.8	6.6	10.5	3.3	2.3	3.1	1.3	1.9	2.1

This same information can be plotted on a graph (Figure 37), showing the possibilities of developing a range of information.

Using graphs such as Figure 37 (see overleaf), coaches should be able to identify the age of PHV onset, the age of PHV itself, and any plateaus in growth.

Table 2 shows the greatest change in stature is 10.5cm per year between the ages of 13.321 and 14.389. Figure 37 shows this in graphical form.

If an average for the age of PHV is taken, it would be approximately 13.9 years.

However, a far more accurate figure can be obtained using a specific calculation (see Appendix 2). When calculating the age of PHV, four variables require consideration:

1. the age centre (average age between two time points) at peak velocity   =   (A)

2. velocity value at peak velocity   =   (VA)

3. velocity one year before peak   =   (VA – 1)

4. velocity one year after peak   =   (VA + 1).

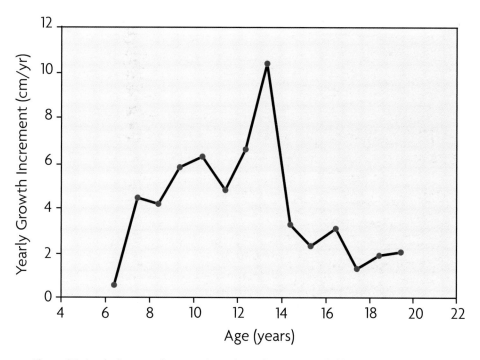

Figure 37: A velocity growth curve of a male performer recorded between the ages of 6–20.

Having considered the variables, the following calculation will determine the age of PHV:

$$\text{Age at peak velocity} = A + \frac{VA - (VA - 1)}{[VA - (VA - 1) + [VA - (VA + 1)]} - 0.5$$

$$= 13.855 + \frac{9.8 - 6.9}{(9.8 - 6.9) + (9.8 - 3.7)} - 0.5$$

$$= 13.855 + 0.32 - 0.5 = \textbf{13.7 years} \ (\textit{13.68 rounded to one decimal place})$$

Therefore, more accurately, the age at PHV for this male performer is 13.7 years.

The advantage of the velocity curve in comparison to the distance curve is that it enables the coach to assess the rate of growth from one point in time to another, against the age of the performer. The velocity curve indicates distinctive growth features to be identified.

These are:

• the onset of the acceleration in the curve

• the peak in the curve and the deceleration of the curve.

Although this curve has peaks and troughs, it is possible to identify the age at which growth was at its highest.

In general, velocity curves are unsuitable to assess three-month measurements, because the graph would consist of a series of mini peaks and troughs and the overall shape of the traditional PHV curve would be unrecognisable.

In principle, a full year's growth is needed to overcome the effects of seasonal variation. Coaches should bear in mind that, on average, about two-thirds of yearly growth occurs in the spring and summer months.

The pattern of annual growth measurement is, in reality, impractical for the coach, who often needs to know if the performer is growing quickly. In this case, the velocity of growth over three months can be obtained by comparing the present measurement to the previous one. This will give an average rate over the specific time period. Secondly, it allows for comparison of the growth at three months to that of the six month increment, before moving on to the nine month increment and, finally, annual velocity. Table 3 offers an example of a girl aged 7.5 years who is measured at three monthly intervals over the course of a year. In each instance, three month, six month, and nine month increments are shown.

Table 3: Stature measurements of a young girl performer and the calculation of annual velocity

Date of Measurement	Decimal Age	Height (cm)	Age Increment	*Age Centre	Simple Velocity (cm)	Annual Velocity
10 September 2005	7.5	123				
			0.25 (three months)			
10 December 2005	7.75	123.5			0.5	
			0.25 (six months)			
8 March 2006	8.162	124.7			1.2	
			0.25 (nine months)			
9 June 2006	8.25	126.1			1.4	
			0.24 (12 months)			
5 September 2006	8.49	128.5			2.4	
			0.99	8.00	5.5	5.6

* Age centre is defined as the average age between two time points.

The interpretation of the final growth point for this girl is important. Table 3 shows in the last three months of measurement, the rate of growth was nearly double of that in the previous three. This indicates the onset of PHV.

It is possible for coaches to use computer programmes such as Microsoft Excel to plot and compute the data in Table 3 on a spreadsheet.

Key Concepts and Summary

- Coaches need to record serial measurements of performers' growth on a quarterly basis.

- Quarterly intervals allow for greater growth than expected from measurement error.

- The more frequently a measurement is taken, the greater the likelihood of error occurring. However, it is recommended to measure on a quarterly basis.

5. Why Measurement Accuracy is Important

The importance of accurate measurement has already been discussed, together with the observance of protocols that help to reduce measurement error. Errors can either be random or measurement specific.

Random error is not systematic and is difficult to detect. Of greater concern is measurement error, which accounts for the largest source of fault in measuring stature. This is why it is important to standardise measurement.

Coaches need to consider the factors that could lead to measurement error. The following list includes some of them:

- The environmental conditions should be considered. The area where testing is taking place should be conducive to obtaining accurate measurements.

- Clothing is important: loose clothing such as training shorts and T-shirts are ideal as they allow the correct body posture for accurate measurement.

- Cooperation of the performers is necessary. Working in smaller groups and bringing the performers to the measuring area reduces the likelihood of error.

6.Other Recommended Measurements

Sitting height and leg length

Sitting height is obtained by measuring the performer in a sitting position. The distance to be measured is from the highest point of the performer to the surface on which the performer is seated (Figure 38).

> The protocol is as follows:
>
> - The measurement of stature should be with the performer's head in the Frankfort plane.
>
> - The hands should be in a relaxed position on the thighs (not on the bench or table).
>
> - The thighs should be in a horizontal position with the back of the knees hanging over the edge of the bench or table, but not in contact with the edge of the seated surface.
>
> - The performer should not be pushing up with their hands or legs.

Instructions given to the performer, the level of accuracy and numbers of recordings should be identical to those used in the measurement of stature.

Once calculated, if sitting height is subtracted from stature, leg length (or subischial height) can be worked out. This score can be important for sports dependent upon knowing leg lengths, such as in cycling, swimming, rowing and gymnastics.

It is possible to apply these principles and techniques to other parts of the body (eg arm length and shoulder width).

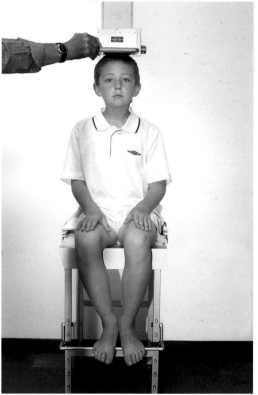

Figure 38: Sitting height photograph

Arm span

Arm span is measured in the standing position with the performer's back against a flat surface, such as a wall. With arms outstretched, measurement is taken from the tip of the longest finger on one hand, to the tip of the finger on the other hand. A tape measure at least 2m long is required.

The protocol is as follows:

- Two measurers are usually required for this procedure. One should hold the zero end of the tape and the other the opposite end against the wall*.

- The performer should stand with feet together and his back against the wall and tape measure.

- Both arms are then outstretched maximally and level with the shoulders. Palms should be facing forwards (eg towards the measurer). The arms should remain in contact with the wall at all times.

- The tip of the longest finger (usually the middle finger) of the right hand is brought into contact with the movable end of the measuring tape, while the same procedure for the left hand is fixed at the zero end of the tape. When recording, testers should exclude long fingernails when measuring from fingertip to fingertip.

- The measurement is recorded to the nearest 0.1cm.

- It is important to ensure the performer's arms are outstretched and do not inadvertently lower. This often occurs with young children.

- Two measurements should be recorded for each performer and these should not differ by more than 0.4cm. If this happens, the average of the two scores is calculated and recorded as the arm span of the performer at that time.

- If measurements differ by more than 0.4cm, a third measurement is required to calculate the median.

---

* In some facilities, a moveable block attached to the wall can act as a fixed perpendicular point to one end of the tape measure. However, in most cases, this is not likely to be available, so measurers must ensure the tape is as horizontal as possible and that one end is fixed perpendicular to either a marked or imaginary point on the wall.

In some cases, if the tester cannot call upon another helper, the points at which the outstretched hands reach can be marked on the wall. Then, the performer can assist the tester to measure the distance between the two points. Best practice would dictate that measurements of this kind should never be undertaken with a child or young person in isolation. Two adults (if necessary one of them the performer's parent) should always be present because of the additional vulnerability of children and young people, particularly where close contact and touch is necessary.

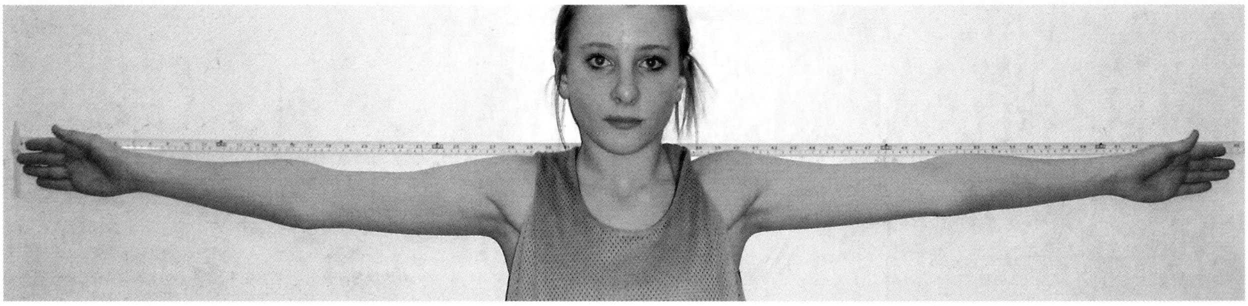

Figure 39: Arm span photograph

Body weight

Peak weight velocity (PWV) is the growth rate of body mass in terms of kilograms in one particular year (kg/yr). PWV typically has its major rate of growth in adolescents about six months after PHV. The major drawback of measuring PWV is that, unlike stature, it is greatly influenced by many factors affecting growth. These include:

- differences in nutrition and the amount of food consumed, which can result in a greater variation in weight than would be experienced in stature

- weight, as it is not just a matter of the absolute weight but comprises both muscle and fat, each of which are changing rapidly in adolescent children.

An increase in weight may, therefore, be an indicator of muscle mass expansion over and above increases in fat, but it may also mean the opposite. Stature measures are more straightforward indicators of growth, because it is solely a measurement of linear height.

Key Concepts and Summary

- Sitting height and leg length are useful measures because they provide specific regional growth patterns, which could be more important to sports such as cycling or gymnastics.

- PWV could also be determined for body mass, but is affected by other factors. Therefore, PWV must be interpreted more carefully than stature measurements.

- Standing height, sitting height and arm span measurements could show the coach which part of the body is growing the fastest (ie legs, trunk or arms). This can help the coach design appropriate fitness or skill development programmes for the performer.

7. Advanced Measurement Techniques

A number of advanced techniques for measurement are available, although they may not always be appropriate for coaches to use.

Salivary testosterone

Hormone markers can be measured in blood serum or saliva. However, the invasive nature of blood sampling by venepuncture is not recommended when working with child athletes. Salivary measurement offers a much easier means of collecting data, as it is a non-invasive method. It requires a child to spit saliva into a collecting tube, the results of which are then analysed at a laboratory for the concentration of different hormone markers.

X-rays

Skeletal maturation (see Chapter 2) is considered the best indicator of biological age or maturity status. This is because it is the only indicator that exists from birth to adulthood. The basis for this method is that a more mature child will have further bone development and less cartilage than an immature child. In order to measure skeletal age, an X-ray is usually taken of the left hand and wrist to assess the amount, shape and contour of bones, and how close they are to achieving adult norms. Because an X-ray is required, this would not be an acceptable technique to use for child performers for the sole purpose of determining maturity status. It should only be used in a clinical situation when there is concern a child is not growing at the appropriate rate. The technique is also expensive, requires access to specialised equipment beyond the facilities of most coaches, and would need a specialist to interpret the results.

8. Ethical and Sensitive Issues

A coach working with young male and female performers must appreciate and understand not only the physical changes to a child's shape and size, but potential implications on personality. The child's perception of his/her body, as well as those of others, are important considerations for coaches. The coach is uniquely placed to offer good advice and educate their performers in a sensitive and appropriate manner. Where a child or young person appears to present a consistently negative body image and low self esteem, it is essential great sensitivity is shown and specialist nutritional or medical advice sought, where appropriate, with the consent of the child's parent/carer. Coaches should always be alert to the limits of their expertise and to any behavioural indicators that a child is distressed or uncomfortable in relation to measuring their growth. Specialist support should be sought and any concerns about a child's welfare (physical or emotional) recorded and reported, in accordance with the sport's governing body procedure.

How a child meets the demands of training and competition structured by the coach is dependent on the interplay between levels and rate of growth, development and maturation of the individual performer. This includes the psychological, emotional and intellectual capability of the child. For many young children, the fear of failing, of actual failure, and of evaluation by others, such as coaches and parents, can be a major cause of stress (Cahill and Pearl, 1993).

Many innovations in sport have tried to reduce these anxieties for young performers. These include modified games such as tag rugby and mini tennis, non-competitive small-sided games, and making equipment that **fits** young children.

The performance advantage early maturity brings to a child will impact significantly on their successful participation in most sports. However, as discussed previously (see Chapter 4), the late maturer often becomes the better performer in the long term.

Finally, the maturational issue is particularly important during adolescent years, when the largest changes in body size and shape take place. Such changes can cause particular concern to females. Peer pressure and a preoccupation with body image have been highlighted for adolescent girls (Otis et al, 1997). Sports emphasising a control of body mass, lean physique and low fatness (body fat), and where competition rules reinforce or reward these factors, are a concern. Such sports include those with a weight category for competition, or where the outcome of a successful performance is partly based on aesthetics. Many of these sports' governing bodies are alert to traditional poor coaching practice relating to weight control, including, for example, 'sweating off' and 'bagging' to reduce weight immediately prior to competition, and have introduced clear practice guidance and sanctions for those found to be continuing such practice.

9. Implications for Coaches

When measuring growth, it is important coaches appreciate and understand the impact of a number of related factors, such as:

- genetics
- nutrition and energy expenditure
- hormones
- epiphyseal (growth plate) injuries
- psychological stress.

Monitoring growth and maturation is only one aspect that influences successful sports participation by children. The factors listed above have an important impact on the success or failure of sporting performance. Coaches **must** appreciate the individuality of children's growth and maturation. They should not favour a particular body shape or size without considering all other factors that impact on the child.

There is little that can be done to influence stature, but young performers are often not selected for teams because they are not strong enough or are too heavy. However, once adulthood has been reached, physical capabilities can be influenced with more structured and intensive training volumes.

More data relating to child athletes from a physiological, psychological and sociological perspective is being acquired and will increase the knowledge base of coaches.

10. Conclusion

The timing and tempo (rate) of children's growth and maturation is highly variable and individualised. Early maturity has advantages for young performers in sports developed in relation to chronological age, so coaches need to be aware of overly concentrating on early maturers. Late maturation does not mean these performers will be poorer when the maturity gap closes between them and early maturers. Many anthropometrical and physiological differences will disappear. Other factors of success, such as skill level and competitiveness, are just as important and are not dependent on growth patterns. Children, young people and their parents also need to be educated to understand these issues, as it can support them to remain motivated and engaged with sports if they can look forward to potentially improved performance and success.

The monitoring of stature will give a general picture of a child's rate of growth and will assist the coach in deciding when training volume, intensity and type could be adjusted. For the interpretation of data to be meaningful, growth measurements need to be collected accurately, and monitored longitudinally, to be of real value in a rapidly changing anthropometrical and physiological system.

Key Concepts and Summary

- Coaches must collect measurement data objectively and resist the temptation to compare one performer with another.
- The measurement of stature must be accurate. An understanding of measurement errors will assist the coach in enhancing the assessment and interpretation of growth patterns.
- By monitoring rapid growth periods, coaches should be able to develop appropriate training programmes during times when the performer might be more prone to injury. The vulnerability chart in Chapter 3, Appendix 5 highlights potential overuse injury issues.
- Averages such as growth velocity at specific ages are often used, but they do not relate to the individual child. The advantage of monitoring each child separately and creating individual growth charts ensures evaluations are meaningful and of benefit.

Appendix 1

The Child Growth Foundation has a dedicated website (www.childgrowthfoundation.org) where growth charts for boys and girls can be purchased. In addition, individual children's data can be entered separately through the website, providing a UK percentile score for stature and body mass measurements.

Appendix 2

Table showing the calculations for increments in age and growth velocity

Decimal Age at Test	Height	Age Increment	Age Centre	Simple Velocity	Annual Velocity
6.45	124	0.99	6.945	0.5	0.5
7.44	124.5	0.959	7.9195	4.5	4.7
8.399	129	0.99	8.894	4.2	4.2
9.389	133.2	0.973	9.8755	5.8	6.0
10.362	139	1.044	10.884	6.3	6.0
11.406	145.3	0.956	11.884	4.8	5.0
12.362	150.1	0.959	12.8415	6.6	6.9
13.321	156.7	1.068	13.855	10.5	9.8
14.389	167.2	0.902	14.84	3.3	3.7
15.291	170.5	1.159	15.8705	2.3	2.0
16.45	172.8	0.956	16.928	3.1	3.2
17.406	175.9	0.993	17.9025	1.3	1.3
18.399	177.2	1.023	18.9105	1.9	1.9
19.422	179.1	1	19.922	2.1	2.1
20.422	181.2				

A = age centre at PHV

VA = velocity value at peak

(VA – 1) = velocity one year before peak

(VA + 1) = velocity one year after peak

$$\text{Age at PHV} = A + \frac{VA - (VA-1)}{[VA-(VA-1)] + [VA-(VA+1)]} - 0.5$$

$$13.855 + \frac{9.8 - 6.9}{(9.8-6.9) + (9.8-3.7)} - 0.5$$

$$13.855 + \frac{2.9}{(2.9+6.1)} - 0.5$$

$$13.855 + 0.32 - 0.5 = 0.5 = \textbf{13.68}$$

The age increment, age centre, simple velocity and annual velocity are calculated as follows. By using the first two lines of data from the above table, the calculations are shown overleaf:

Age increment = decimal age at test 2 subtracted from test 1

Age increment = 7.44 – 6.45 = 0.99 years

Age centre = the sum of the decimal age at test 2 and test 1 divided by 2

Age centre = (7.44 + 6.45) / 2 = 6.945 years

Simple velocity = the subtraction of the stature measurement of test 2 from test 1

Simple velocity = 124.5 – 124 = 0.5cm

Annual velocity = the simple velocity sum divided by the sum of the age increment sum

Annual velocity = 0.5 / 0.99 = 0.5cm

This calculation is then repeated between data rows 3 and 2, 4 and 3, 5 and 4 etc.

Appendix 3

Calculation of decimal age

To calculate the decimal age of a performer, use the table below to decimalise the date of measurement and the performer's date of birth. For example, a performer measured on 25 March 2006, whose birthdate is 20 January 1996, would be calculated as follows:

25 March equates to 0.227 of the year and 20 January to 0.052. As there are 10 complete chronological years between the two dates, the remainder is simply a subtraction between the **measurement data** and the **birth date**: 0.227 – 0.052 = 0.175. Therefore, add the total chronological years (10) with the current decimal year age (0.175) and the performer's decimal age is 10.175 years.

	1 Jan	2 Feb	3 Mar	4 Apr	5 May	6 Jun	7 Jul	8 Aug	9 Sept	10 Oct	11 Nov	12 Dec
1	000	085	162	247	329	414	496	581	666	748	833	915
2	003	088	164	249	332	416	499	584	668	751	836	918
3	005	090	167	252	334	419	501	586	671	753	838	921
4	008	093	170	255	337	422	504	589	674	756	841	923
5	011	096	173	258	340	425	507	592	677	759	844	926
6	014	099	175	260	342	427	510	595	679	762	847	929
7	016	101	178	263	345	430	512	597	682	764	849	932
8	019	104	181	266	348	433	515	600	685	767	852	934
9	022	107	184	268	351	436	518	603	688	770	855	937
10	025	110	186	271	353	438	521	605	690	773	858	940
11	027	112	189	274	356	441	523	608	693	775	860	942
12	030	115	192	277	359	444	526	611	696	778	863	945
13	033	118	195	279	362	447	529	614	699	781	866	948
14	036	121	197	282	364	449	532	616	701	784	868	951
15	038	123	200	285	367	452	534	619	704	786	871	953
16	041	126	203	288	370	455	537	622	707	789	874	956
17	044	129	205	290	373	458	540	625	710	792	877	959
18	047	132	208	293	375	460	542	627	712	795	879	962
19	049	134	211	296	378	463	545	630	715	797	882	964
20	052	137	214	299	381	466	548	633	718	800	885	967
21	055	140	216	301	384	468	551	636	721	803	888	970
22	058	142	219	304	386	471	553	638	723	805	890	973
23	060	145	222	307	389	474	556	641	726	808	893	975
24	063	148	225	310	392	477	559	644	729	811	896	978
25	066	151	227	312	395	479	562	647	731	814	899	981
26	068	153	230	315	397	482	564	649	734	816	901	984
27	071	156	233	318	400	485	567	652	737	819	904	986
28	074	159	236	321	403	488	570	655	740	822	907	989
29	077		238	323	405	490	573	658	742	825	910	992
30	079		241	326	408	493	575	660	745	827	912	995
31	082		244		411		578	663		830		997

References

Cahill, B.R. and Pearl, A.J. (1993) *Intensive Participation in Children's Sports*. Leeds: Human Kinetics Europe Ltd. ISBN: 978-0-880116-98-5.

Freeman, J.V., Cole, T.J., Chinn, S., Jones, P.R.M., White, E.M., Preece, M.A. (1995) 'Cross-sectional stature and weight reference curves for the UK', *Archives of Disease in Childhood*, 1990, 73: 17–24.

Mirwald, R.L., Baxter-Jones, A.D., Bailey, D.A. and Beunen, G.P. (2002) 'An assessment of maturity from anthropometric measurements', *Medicine and Science in Sports and Exercise*, 34 (4): 689–94.

Otis, C.L., Drinkwater, B., Johnson, M., Loucks, A. and Wilmore, J. (1997) 'The female performer triad: American College of Sports Medicine position stand', *Medicine and Science in Sports and Exercise*, 29, 1–ix.

Tanner J., Whitehouse, R. and Takaishi, M. (1966a) 'Standards from birth to maturity for height weight, height velocity and weight velocity: British children 1965 Part I', *Archives of Disease in Childhood*, 41: 457–471.

Tanner J., Whitehouse, R., Takaishi, M. (1966b) 'Standards from birth to maturity for height weight, height velocity and weight velocity: British children 1965 Part II', *Archives of Disease in Childhood*, 41: 613–635.

Further Reading

Armstrong N. and Van Mechelen, W. (2008) *Paediatric exercise science and medicine* (second edition). Oxford: Oxford University Press. ISBN: 978-0-199232-48-2.

Falgariette, G., Bedu, M., Fellmann, N., Van-Praagh, E. and Coudert, J. (1991). 'Bio-energetic profile in 144 boys aged from 6 to 15 years with special reference to sexual maturation', *European Journal of Applied Physiology*, 62: 151–156.

Malina, R.M., Bouchard, C. and Bar-Or, O. (2004) *Growth, maturation and physical activity*. Champaign, Illinois: Human Kinetics. ISBN: 978-0-880118-82-8.

Williams, C.A. (1995) *Anaerobic performance of prepubescent and adolescent children*. (unpublished PhD thesis, University of Exeter).

Chapter 7: **Conclusion**

Ian Stafford

Coaches of quality programmes for young performers should now be ready to use the information in this resource in their planning and coaching. This chapter reviews the previous material and summarises the overall key messages.

Before doing so, it is useful to have a final recap on the content and messages of the individual chapters.

Chapter 1 built on the introduction outlined in the Preface and set the scene for the chapters that follow. It reviewed the core values and key principles of LTAD and provided some background context in relation to the role and responsibilities of coaches, in supporting overall health and well-being of young performers, as well as guiding their improvement within a particular sport. It highlighted LTAD as an evolving framework and the unique nature of this resource as the first of its kind.

Chapter 2 covered patterns and key terms in growth and development. It examined the differences between male and female growth patterns and set out methods of monitoring growth and development. The importance and use of measurements of growth in coaching was covered, and key issues relating to ethical practice and sensitivity were addressed. Key messages:

- Coaches working with young, developing performers need to understand the key aspects of growth and development in order to use the indicators and also have a monitoring process that informs their programming.

- Measurement should be an integral part of ongoing profiling/testing or at least be part of an annual, or more frequent, medical check-up.

- Coaches and support teams should begin to rationalise their approaches to training, based on the monitoring information and estimated maturity status of individual, young performers.

- The adoption of simple procedures will enable coaches to plan and adjust the training, competition and recovery programme, according to the individual development of each young performer.

Chapter 3 provided an overview of adaptation and trainability. It discussed the concept of windows of trainability and the trainability of aerobic, strength, speed, skill and suppleness capabilities. Key messages:

- Coaches should ensure the programmes of their young performers, in terms of training, competition and recovery, are appropriate to each individual's growth, development and maturation needs.

- Training gains offered by using windows of trainability for the five Ss of training and performance provide coaches with a method of working, which ultimately supports performers in their ability to fulfil their potential.

- Periodised training, competition and recovery programmes for young developing performers should be adapted to meet the needs of the individual and the demands of the sport, as soon as the coach is able to monitor patterns of growth, development and maturation.

Chapter 4 examined several issues of concern to coaches who want to develop quality training and competition programmes for young performers. It discussed the concepts of early and late specialisation, relative age and early and late maturation. It then set out the progressive phases of growth. Key messages:

- An understanding of the implications of early and late maturation and the relative age effect is important, because the way in which coaches reflect these in their planning may influence whether young performers stay in the sport or reach their potential.

- Monitoring of biological markers throughout phases of growth and using identified measurements should guide the coach in optimising specific training for the young developing performer.

- Effective coaches will be aware of the issues raised in this chapter and take them into account in their planning, training and competitive processes.

Chapter 5 focused on case studies from women's football and tennis. These studies showed how the two sports have incorporated the processes and complexities of growth, development and maturation of young players into the planning of quality and relevant coaching programmes for the first three stages of LTAD. Key messages:

- Sensitive windows of trainability were identified for both sports for each stage.

- Many similarities were evident between the studies, despite the fact football and tennis are very different sports.

- Similarities arise from the fact both sports are working with the same age groups of players as they move through their careers. Young performers are individuals first and sports performers second.

- Differences arise from the team or individual nature of the sport, and the seasonality of football and the all-year-round nature of tennis.

- The importance of developing individual factors of the 10 Ss at different stages cannot be overestimated, because they link closely to the sensitive windows of trainability and biological markers for young players.

- With careful integration of individual factors, coaches in both sports should be able to develop young players to their full potential.

Chapter 6 examined the tools and equipment for measurement. It explained the importance of accurate measurements and set out the procedures, protocols and timings for recording them. It discussed both basic and advanced measurements, as well as important ethical issues. Key messages:

- Coaches need to collect objective data and resist the temptation to compare one performer with another.

- The measurement of stature must be accurate. An understanding of measurement errors will assist the coach in enhancing the assessment and interpretation of growth patterns.

- Monitoring periods of growth in young performers enables coaches to develop appropriate training programmes during the times when the performer might be more prone to injury.

- Monitoring each performer separately, to create individual growth charts, ensures evaluations are meaningful and valuable for the individual performer. Averages such as growth velocity at specific ages are often used, but they do not relate to every child.

Structured, progressive and developmentally appropriate preparation programmes are advantageous for all young people who participate in sport. However, for those who progress through to the higher levels of performance, to achieve success and realise their potential as more senior performers, the nature of this preparation and progression becomes vital to the achievement of their goals.

The role of the coach is fundamental. When working with young performers, coaches will generally play a more prominent role in planning and organising training, competition and recovery programmes, than they will when working with more experienced and knowledgeable adult performers, whose programmes are more likely to be the result of discussion and negotiation.

The coach plays an essential role in developing programmes that encourage achievement in young performers. Achievement fosters self-esteem and all coaches of children and young people, regardless of the level at which they coach, have a role to play in fostering positive youth development. Especially at the higher levels of performance, the personal attributes of high self-confidence and positive self-esteem are qualities that coaches want to develop in all of their young performers. It is difficult to imagine a young performer being able to attain and maintain high levels of performance without a real belief in their own capabilities, and without the high levels of self-confidence such belief instils. This level of self-confidence will rarely, if ever, be fostered in young performers who constantly fail to achieve because of inappropriate goals or training programmes.

Coaches of children and young people will be much more likely to set appropriate goals and training programmes if they understand how their young athletes grow, develop and mature, and the implications that these processes have for their coaching. This resource provides relevant references to help coaches develop a deeper understanding of young performers. It was identified from the outset that, at the higher performance levels, coaches will need to know about periodisation to break the preparation and competitive programme down into appropriate and progressive phases.

The specific focus of this resource has been on tracking the physical development of young performers and then using the information obtained to design and implement effective and meaningful coaching programmes. As stated in Chapter 1, this does not mean the physical development of young performers is any more important than the psychological, social or emotional capabilities coaches should take into account when developing programmes, or in their face-to-face coaching. It is worth stating that factors such as developing skills or fostering a real will-to-win may be as important ingredients in producing a successful performer as physical conditioning and development.

However, physical growth and development are more readily accessible to direct measuring, assessment and tracking than other aspects of maturation, such as psychological and social skills. Growth, development and maturation, and specifically the onset of PHV and PHV itself, are relatively easy to understand and can be used by many coaches to inform the design and implementation of programmes.

While acknowledging the practical constraints, coaches are urged to adopt an approach to the programme of training, competition and recovery for young, developing performers on a basis that reflects the individual's appropriate developmental considerations. This is fundamental to the subsequent development and ultimate performance levels of the individual performer.

Key considerations include:

- early and late maturation

- gender of the performer

- relative age.

Each of these factors can have a significant impact on both the chances of keeping young people actively participating in sport, and on the likelihood of young performers developing to their true potential. Busy coaches working with talent identified or high-level young performers should continue to remind themselves of the principles and considerations at the very heart of what they are doing and working towards. At this level, it is all too easy to be fully occupied by organisational demands and forget that coaches are charged with the important responsibility of helping young people fulfil their dreams and ambitions. This is obviously not a short-term activity. Coaches working with children and young people need to plan for long-term investment to reap real rewards, because they must chart the progress of their promising young athletes through to becoming successful senior performers.

As in all references to the current LTAD model, a strong reminder is provided that this model is not set in stone and has continuous improvement enshrined in its philosophy. Coaches may be aware of the addition of the Active Start phase and have noticed the change in the name of the Learning to Train stage to Learning to Play and Practice. These are just two simple examples of the evolution within the model, so a plea is made to all coaches to remain up to date in terms of their knowledge. This should also apply to the skills of a coach, which need to be constantly honed and reviewed. A commitment to continuous improvement must be one of the professional responsibilities of every coach, if the status of coaching is to be raised and professionalised.

Coaching the Young Developing Performer has been written with the explicit aim of helping coaches and support staff to give young, competitive performers the best deal. It is certainly easier to devise and coach a general programme where all performers of a specific age group experience much the same preparation, competition and recovery schedules, but this will not give future high-level performers what they require. If the card game analogy is continued, the chances of performers winning when they have been dealt the best hand, is much greater. Thus, the role of the coach in helping young performers achieve the best deal will be crucial in determining ultimate performance levels and success.

The link has been made between what coaches of young people are doing now and preparation ahead of the London 2012 Olympic Games and Paralympic Games and the Commonwealth Games in Glasgow in 2014. The simple message is this: A gymnastics coach working with 10–12 year olds, or an athletics coach working with 16–18 year olds, needs to be putting many of the lessons given in this resource in place now. For all coaches working with young performers who have aspirations to be there and achieve in high-level competition, the same message applies.

Coaching the Young Developing Performer has been targeted at coaches working with children and young people at the higher performance levels. Although it is intended to be specifically relevant for this level of coaching, there is much within the resource from which other coaches and support staff should be able to learn.

In the UK at present, education and sport rely almost exclusively on the categorisation of young people under 18 years of age by chronological age. Whereas the attraction of this as a simple and generally effective approach can be appreciated, the shortcomings of any system that relies on chronological divisions (especially during puberty) can now be understood. Coaches with experience of coaching children and young people and/or who have read the literature on child development, will already be aware of the individual differences that exist in terms of rates of growth and development. This can be particularly evident in the early teenage years, as was discussed in Chapter 4, where a group of 13 year olds may have a developmental age range of four years.

It has been stated many times in this resource that individual differences in the rate and stage of development must be carefully monitored and accounted for in training programmes. However, attention should also be drawn to the dangers of categorising children and young people simply on the basis of developmental age and stage. The role of the coach is to help develop young people **in** sport and **through** sport. Separating young people from their age group peers **for all activities** because, developmentally, they are operating at an advanced or delayed rate (an early or a late maturer) will impact on their social development. So, coaches need to strike a careful balance between the needs of the young performer in terms of both their sport development and their overall personal development. This may present a significant challenge for coaches, but if the challenge is met successfully, the rewards to be gained from playing a central role in the development of young people, both as performers and as individuals, can be well worth it…in the long run.

Glossary

Adolescence

This is a difficult period to define in terms of its onset and termination. During this period, most bodily systems become adult both structurally and functionally. Structurally, adolescence begins with an acceleration in the rate of growth spurt. The rate of statural growth reaches its peak, begins a slower or decelerative phase, and finally terminates with the attainment of adult stature. Functionally, adolescence is usually viewed in terms of sexual maturity, which begins with changes in the neuroendocrine system prior to overt physical changes, and terminates with the attainment of mature reproductive function.

Adolescent growth spurt (circumpubertal period)

The adolescent growth spurt that lasts up to four-and-a-half years.

Adulthood

The period of time in life after physical growth has stopped and an individual becomes fully developed.

Aerobic power

The highest work rate or power output at which energy can be produced aerobically.

Anaerobic alactic power

The rate at which energy can be released by phosphagens (ATP-CP system) during a supramaximal effort. It is usually assessed from peak power output reached during all-out efforts from rest, lasting less than one to five seconds.

Biological age

A variable age that corresponds roughly to chronological age, determined by measures of morphological, skeletal, dental or sexual age.

Biological markers

Biological markers can be described as key events during the adolescence growth spurt, such as the onset of PHV, PHV itself, and the onset of menarche. These markers provide coaches with key indicators as to what stage an individual is at during their growth spurt. In turn, these indicators can provide guidance to coaches as to when and why to change the nature of the training stimuli, to optimise performance potential.

Biological maturity

A means by which an evaluation of biological maturity is made using maturity criteria, such as measures of morphological, skeletal, dental or sexual age.

Chronological age

This refers to the number of years and days elapsed since birth. Growth, development and maturation operate in a time framework – the child's chronological age. Children of the same chronological age differ by several years in their level of biological maturation. The integrated nature of growth and maturation is achieved by the interaction of genes, hormones, nutrients and the physical and psychosocial environments in which the individual lives. This complex interaction regulates the child's growth, neuromuscular maturation, sexual maturation and general physical metamorphosis during the first two decades of life.

Early childhood

This ordinarily spans from the end of infancy (the first birthday) to the start of adolescence and is characterised by relatively steady progress in growth and maturation, and rapid progress in neuromuscular or motor development. Early childhood includes pre-school children aged 1–5 years.

Early and late maturity

Early maturation refers to when an individual's biological development is at an advanced stage, compared to the average biological development for an individual of a certain chronological age. Late maturation is where an individual's biological development is in a less advanced stage, compared to the average biological development for an individual of a certain chronological age. In general terms, while each growth spurt is different in terms of its duration and tempo, those individuals that start their growth spurt earlier than the average age for the onset of PHV, tend to be referred to as early maturers. Individuals who start their growth spurt later than the average age for the onset of PHV, tend to be referred to as late maturers.

Early and late specialisation sports

Sports can be broadly categorised as either early or late specialisation in terms of differing training requirements. Examples of early specialisation sports include gymnastics, diving, figure skating and table tennis. The nature of these sports, in terms of developing high-level performers, demands a much earlier sport-specific specialisation in preparation programmes. Most sports, with a few notable exceptions, are late specialisation. In these more common sports, a more generalised approach is beneficial in the early stages of development. In these early stages of late specialisation sports, the most FUNdamental movement skills should be developed, alongside a basic technical and tactical awareness involving a range of activities/sports.

Growth

An increase in the size of the body and its parts.

Infancy

The early stage of growth and development.

Kinanthropometry

This is the area of science concerned with the measurement of human body composition. As a result of alterations in lifestyle, nutrition, activity levels and ethnic composition of populations, changes to the distribution of body dimensions are forever occurring. Kinanthropometry is the interface between anatomy and movement. It takes the measurement of the human body and determines its capability for function and movement in a range of settings.

Maturation

A process of developmental change characterised by a fixed order of progression, in which pace may vary but sequence of appearance of characteristics generally does not. Coming to full development equals becoming mature.

Menarche

The first menstrual flow of an adolescent female.

Middle childhood

During middle childhood, children grow at a slow and consistent rate. The average weight increase is about 5–7lbs per year. Muscle mass increases as baby fat decreases, legs become longer and the trunk slimmer. In addition, strength increases while motor skills become smoother and more coordinated.

Overcompensation

This is a state of increased work capacity or ability to tolerate stress above the levels recently attainable. Overcompensation is observed as a result of the administration of a training stimulus, followed by appropriate recovery conditions.

Peak height velocity (PHV)

PHV is the maximum rate of growth in stature during growth spurt. The age of maximum velocity of growth is called the age at PHV. The onset of PHV refers to the age when growth spurt occurs (see Chapter 2, Figure 2).

Peak weight velocity (PWV)

PWV is the maximum rate of increase in weight during growth spurt. The age of maximum increase in weight is called the age at PWV.

Periodisation

Periodisation is the structuring or cycling of short- and/or long-term training programmes to provide optimum performance(s) at the required time(s) or time series. The term is a synonym for planning for athletic training and performance. In order to attain peak performance, training must be arranged so the athlete achieves a simultaneous peak in all components of training, including physical, mental, technical and tactical skills. Nutritional, medical and environmental factors, and equipment, must also be optimised. Coaches are responsible for the planning and implementation process involved in achieving peak performance. Therefore, they must carefully integrate and sequence all the factors of training and performance.

Readiness

This refers to a child's level of growth, maturity and development that enables him/her to perform tasks and meet demands through training and competition. Readiness and critical periods of trainability during growth and development of young athletes are also referred to as the correct time for the programming of certain stimuli to achieve optimum adaptation, with regards motor skills, muscular and/or aerobic power.

Relative age effect

The relative age effect describes the observation that greater numbers of performers born early in a selection year are overrepresented in junior and senior elite squads, compared with what might be expected based on national birthrates (Sportnation: A Sporting Chance www.thelssa.co.uk/lssa/sportnation/Sportnation2006.asp).

Sensitive periods of trainability

These are broad time frames for development of a specific ability or capability that go beyond the narrow view of the critical period hypothesis.

Sexual maturation

Puberty refers to the point at which an individual is sexually mature and able to reproduce.

Skeletal maturation

Skeletal age refers to the maturity of the skeleton, determined by the degrees of ossification of bone structure. It's a measure of age that takes into consideration how far bones have progressed towards maturity, not in size, but with regards shape and position with others.

Windows of opportunity

Refers to time periods coinciding with the windows of trainability (see below), which offer coaches the opportunity to prioritise certain training stimuli to optimise the development of certain performance capabilities.

Windows of trainability

The sensitive periods of accelerated adaptation to training, which occur prior to, during and early post-puberty. These windows of trainability are fully open during the sensitive periods of accelerated adaptation to training, and partially open outside of the sensitive periods.

Mission Statement

sports coach UK is dedicated to guiding the development and implementation of a coaching system, recognised as a world leader, for all coaches at every level in the UK.

We will work with our partners to achieve this, by promoting:

- professional and ethical values
- inclusive and equitable practice
- agreed national standards of competence as a benchmark at all levels
- a regulated and licensed structure
- recognition, value and appropriate funding and reward
- a culture and structure of innovation, constant renewal and continuous professional development (CPD).